LUCY CAVENDISH COLLEGE
CAMBRIDGE

A history of the early years

by

C Kate Bertram, J.P., M.A., Ph.D.

Past President and
Honorary Fellow of the College

Cambridge 1989

Errata

Please add cross references as follows:

Page 9 paragraph 3 line 14 insert "page 6".

Page 20 paragraph 3 line 4 insert "page 28".

Page 27 paragraph 1 line 3 insert "page 23"

Page 45 paragraph 1 line 21 insert "page 49".

Page 49 paragraph 1 line 1 insert "page 45".

Page 58 paragraph line 4 insert "page 50".

Page 59 paragraph line 2 insert "page 40".

Page 64 paragraph line 5 insert "page 60".

Page 65 paragraph 3 and 5 delete references.

Page 67 paragraph 0 insert "page 74".

Page 72 paragraph insert "page 55".

The errors listed on th
_____ .ne fault of the author

1__ transferred and typeset by
PCS Typesetting, Frome, Somerset

Printed in Great Britain by
Hillman Printers (Frome) Ltd, Frome, Somerset

LUCY CAVENDISH COLLEGE CAMBRIDGE

A history of the early years

by

C Kate Bertram, J.P., M.A., Ph,D.
Past President and Honorary Fellow of the College
Cambridge 1989

ORDER FORM

To: The Recorder, Lucy Cavendish College.

Please send me _____ copies of C Kate Bertram's 'Lucy Cavendish College'
Hardback £6; paper £5; p&p £1.50.

I enclose cheque/PO for £_____

NAME_____(BLOCK CAPITALS PLEASE)

ADDRESS_____

_____

_____Signature_____

Kate Bertram (née Ricardo), retired from the Presidency of the College in 1979. She is a Zoologist, whose early work was upon the fish and fisheries of Central Africa. She travelled widely there in the thirties with a Newnham colleague and then served in Palestine during the war with her husband Colin, also a Zoologist and later to become Senior Tutor of St. John's College. Together they travelled far studying the Sirenia (Seacows), an endangered mammal. They have four sons and twelve grandchildren.

Kate Bertram sat as a magistrate on the Cambridgeshire Bench for twenty years.

She has personal knowledge of the three other women's colleges, having been an undergraduate at Newnham, a research student at Girton and a member of the first Council of New Hall. She is, perhaps, uniquely well qualified to write a history of the early days of the fourth and youngest women's college, Lucy Cavendish College.

CONTENTS

CONTENTS

FOREWORD

No one could be better qualified than Kate Bertram to undertake the task of recording the origins and early growth of Lucy Cavendish College. Her careful and loving account, complete except in giving credit for her own major role, will be read with nostalgia by those who shared in the formative years. For later comers to the College, this history provides an insight into the thinking which inspired its foundation as well as recounting the labours required to get it launched. It was often a hard road and required much devoted effort. But members of the Dining Group, joined by a growing body of supporters within and beyond the University, were sustained by their keenly perceived concept of helping older women wishing to work and study here. Beginning with women already employed in academic work but wanting a College as a focal point, their efforts soon encompassed the needs of graduates and then of mature women undergraduates. These have remained the twin concerns of the College. Happily, the cause of older women in academic life is much more widely recognised and supported today than it was in 1965 and the "pre-history" years recorded here. We can be confident that the College will continue to show the flexibility and the vision to meet changing needs. It has an immediate and key role to play in helping mature women to develop their abilities to the full at a time when the country – and notably industry and the professions – faces a growing skills shortage.

The history appears as the College approaches its 25th Jubilee year. That is a time when any institution is entitled to think of itself as permanent and to want a record of its past history. That Lucy Cavendish is here to stay is clear not only from its formal status as an Approved Foundation of the University (since 1984) but also from the expansion of accommodation as, statutory quota removed (1988), we embark on increasing student numbers. Legislative provision (1989) will allow the College to continue to offer its unique support to mature women, both students and academics. The Fellowship today is at one with the Founding Fellows in wishing to preserve the special role of the College in furthering the academic work of its members and the College's special quality of friendly supportiveness.

As the years pass, this history will keep new generations in touch with the spirit as well as the aims of the Founding Fellows. This is as it should be, for

> "Time present and time past
> are both present in time future" (T S Eliot)

Anne Warburton
President
February 1989

INTRODUCTION

When I retired as President of Lucy Cavendish College, I offered to write an account of its origins and history. The College agreed that such an account was needed and that it should be written soon before too many of its Founding Fellows disappeared. I was therefore invited to go ahead and prepare one. This I have done and I should like here to thank all those who have helped me. The names of some of these appear in the text, mainly in connection with particular items. Some names are in the notes and appendices, and some there be, which have no memorial but whose contribution is quite as great.

I have deliberately called this account "A History", the "A" is included to indicate that, where views are expressed, they are mine alone. However by far the greatest part of the text is purely factual and contains frequent quotations from the Cambridge Reporter, the official journal of the University. All other references to published works are included in the notes, but the main sources of most of the data are the records of the College itself during a period of over thirty years. The earliest records needed considerable detective work to get them into chronological order, for, as so often happens in new societies, too many papers were undated and bore no initials. Therefore it was much more satisfactory for someone who had been there since the beginning, such as myself, to sort them than for a later historian to undertake the task. The later records are contained in the minutes of the meetings of the College's Trustees and Governing Body. Though the history is as accurate as I can make it, I cannot help bearing in mind the little rhyme about minutes which says:

> The Cabinet rises and goes to its dinner,
> The Secretary stays and gets thinner and thinner,
> Scratching his brains to record and report
> What he thinks that they think they ought to have thought.

Quoted in a letter to The Times on 20/1/1985.

A HISTORY OF LUCY CAVENDISH COLLEGE

I. Before Recognition by the University – 1950–1965

1. Primarily Background

"We are the kind of people who could be used to make the nucleus of a new College in Cambridge." This was said around 1950 by one of three women who had recently come to lunch together each week at Toni's Restaurant[1] in Cambridge. The three then "ordered three glasses of wine and drank to the new project". Little did they know that, fifteen years and many vicissitudes later, their vision would become a reality.

Before describing how this came about, we should look back at Cambridge in the years shortly after the Second World War. The University was full to overflowing with undergraduates. As well as the normal annual intake, there were also all those returning from war service. The colleges were stretched to capacity; St. John's, for example, had a maximum of 800 instead of its former 500 and the women's colleges, whose numbers were strictly limited by the University, were allowed temporarily to expand from 500 to 580, (University Reporter 1945/6, p.298).

It was a lively and invigorating time, for the presence of older men and women among the undergraduate population added much to the variety and interest of Cambridge life. It was, perhaps, the first taste that many College Tutors had had of 'mature students' and they liked it. They were sorry when the average age of undergraduates dropped again and almost all came straight from school. Numbers however did not fall back to pre-war levels and soon began to increase steadily each year until quite recent times. This steady increase in student numbers was the result of R.A. Butler's Education Act of 1944. This far-sighted Act, published in some of the darkest days of the war, requires local authorities to provide secondary education for all its pupils. (In 1939 only 14% of the nation's children were receiving secondary education.)

---

1 Later to become Millers and now Heffer's Bookshop.

1

The provision of universal secondary education, together with a system of maintenance grants, resulted in a largely increased number of boys and girls in the 1950s being able to consider going to a university. To cope with this increase there was a large crop of new universities in the country following the Robbins Report in 1963. In Cambridge the rise in student numbers continued until it was halted in 1976 when the University decided that, both for its own good and for that of the city, there should be no further increase in size. Cambridge was to become a 'steady-state' university rather than an expanding one.

During the period of rapid expansion, it was a major problem for the colleges to cope with the rise in the numbers of students, both graduate and undergraduate. Most felt that they had already reached an optimum size, the optima depending on their buildings, their endowment and their traditions. So there was at that time much talk about the need for new colleges in Cambridge when our three women began to lunch and talk together in 1950.

The years succeeding the Second World War saw a resurgence of the movement, initiated in the 1860s and '70s, to secure greater rights and opportunities for women. The militant suffragettes under Mrs. Pankhurst from 1908–1914 may be thought of as a pressure group within that campaign. After the 1914–18 war, women obtained the vote and many doors were opened to them in the professions and in industry. They entered parliament, and in a variety of ways made their contribution to public life, in spite of persistent opposition from some quarters. Even recently introduced legislation, aimed at combating discrimination against women, has sometimes produced results directly opposite to those intended, because of the complexities involved. It was after the Second World War that the University of Cambridge began to consider how to improve the position of its academic women.

Although women had lived and worked in Cambridge colleges since the 1880s when Girton and Newnham were founded, they were, until 1947, outside rather than a part of the University. As early as 1880 the University considered "the encouragement to be given to the Higher Education of Women". As a result, although they were not to be awarded degrees, 'female students' were to be allowed to take the Tripos examinations and their results were to be published in class lists at the same time and in the same form as those of "the members of the University" (Reporter 1880/81, p.194). Forty years later, in 1920, the University again considered women and their relationship to the University. Alternative proposals were put forward: the first that women should be admitted to membership on the same conditions as men, and the second that the status of women should be unchanged, but they should be awarded 'Titular Degrees'. Sadly the first proposal was rejected and the second chosen by a large majority of votes (Reporter 1920/21, p.902 & 907). The title of a degree was still all that we, in my generation at Newnham, could gain and our certificates were sent by post and without any ceremony. However, these certificates, perhaps in compensation for the real

2

thing, did have a small pale blue bow of ribbon attached which the men did not have!

Although the titular degree, I understand, gave the right to wear gowns, the women agreed, as a matter of courtesy, not to wear them in Cambridge. However, the concession was much valued by schoolteachers and others who were then able to wear academic dress alongside women from other universities. Fortunately there were a few advantages in not being members of the University. For example we did not come under the jurisdiction of the Proctors and we could go to the gallery of the Festival Theatre where we could get seats for half the price that our male friends had to pay in the circle (i.e. sixpence instead of a shilling). Nonetheless we were outsiders which was somewhat uncomfortable even for undergraduates. For senior women the position was far more serious and there was much that was frustrating. Even though they could hold the highest teaching posts in the University, they could take no share in the final decisions made by the University either on general policy or on matters in their own faculties. They could read in the University Library, but could not take books out unless they had a slip signed by a male colleague.

The first move after the Second World War was made in 1946 by two Fellows of King's College, a college with a record of kindness in helping women's colleges. They presented a Memorial to the University signed by 142 of its senior members. The Memorial opened by stating "Twenty-five years have elapsed since the present system was adopted whereby members of the women's colleges have virtually all the rights and duties of members of the University, save those of actual membership. The signatories to this Memorial, which has been prepared without the knowledge of the women's colleges, believe that the question of women's membership should now be reconsidered . . . "It also pointed out that there were, at that time, "two women who are Professors and twenty who are University Lecturers; two women are heads of departments; and women serve as members of many faculties, boards and syndicates . . . "It emphasised that "to deprive some of the teaching officers of ultimate responsibility appears to be contrary to the principle of self-government in the University of Cambridge". Finally it asked for a syndicate to be set up to consider the matter "and to report to the University at an early date" (Reporter 1946/47, p.269).

A syndicate was at once established under the chairmanship of Mr. E.A. Benians, then Master of St. John's, another college which has given much help to women's colleges in Cambridge. At the end of 1947 the syndicate recommended that women should be admitted to membership of the University with a limitation of numbers (Reporter 1946/47, p.1083). There were a large number of women present as spectators when this recommendation was put to the University in a congregation. Apparently, after the reading of the

3

Grace, there was a long, breathless silence and when the word "placet" was heard there was a great gasp of relief. The recommendation was subsequently approved by the King in Council in April 1948, and Cambridge, although the last university in Britain to do so, admitted women to its membership. It had taken it 27 years longer than Oxford to take this dangerous step.

The decision caused much jubilation and women received a wonderful welcome. Celebrations were held in the colleges and, newly-clad in our academic gowns, we rejoiced. I have heard memories of a splendid dinner in King's College,[3] and a future President of Lucy Cavendish and I both recall a delightful reception in St. John's from which, in Anna Bidder's words, "we went home in a soft rosy glow after excellent punch". She also says that to those of her generation the warmth of this general welcome gave particular pleasure after the long period of being on sufferance.

The new status certainly aroused further interest in women's university education in Cambridge. The limitation in numbers provoked much discussion during which it was pointed out that Cambridge in 1950 had a lower proportion of women undergraduates than any other university in the country. The proportion of female to male undergraduates was just under 10%, whereas it was nearly 20% in Oxford and 23% nationally. So, while considering the need for new colleges in general, there was talk of a special need for a new college for women. It was against this background that Margaret Braithwaite made her seminal remark about those at the weekly lunches possibly becoming the nucleus of such a new college.

2.   A Third Women's College

The women who started the Thursday lunches were members of Newnham College. They were Margaret Braithwaite (née Masterman), M.A., a philosopher and later Director of the Cambridge Language Research Unit, and Kathleen Wood-Legh, D.Litt., an eminent mediaeval historian. They were immediately joined by Anna Bidder, Ph.D., a zoologist, later to become Curator of Malacology in the Museum of Zoology. All three were teaching and doing research in the University, but none had continuing close connection with their former college. This resulted in a feeling of some isolation, accentuated by blindness in the case of K. Wood-Legh, and the care of small children or of an aged parent in the cases of the others. They lacked most of the feed-back and involvement normally found in academic life. So stimulating did they find the opportunity to discuss their work and University affairs that they sought out their colleagues whom they believed would share

3 Mrs Barbara White, then Bursar of Newnham College.

their views and hopes.[4] Some of these remained members of the group indefinitely while others drifted away. However, the group grew in number and, as more scientists joined, the time of the weekly meetings was changed to the evenings, for the demands of laboratory work made lengthy lunch-time discussion impossible.

I was first taken to meet this group early in 1951 and soon began dining with them regularly. At this time we were thinking in terms of a new ordinary undergraduate college for women. As soon as we seriously started to formulate our ideas as to how such a college could be founded, we realised that our group would have to become more organised if it were to have any influence. As a first step it seemed wise to decide on criteria for its membership and, on advice, we agreed to limit it to those women who were members of the Regent House, in effect the body responsible for the government of the University, (see Appendix I). The advice to make the membership of our group contingent on membership of the Regent House was wise for it ensured that selection would be objective and not subjective.[5]

Only those who had already been selected on academic grounds by the University or the colleges could join.[6]

In order to prevent the membership becoming impractically large, we agreed that women who already held fellowships in other colleges should not be included. The reason for this was that such women had plenty of opportunities for meeting academic colleagues and having a say in University matters. Thus our group became known as the 'Society of Women Members of the Regent House who are not Fellows of Colleges'. Clearly so cumbersome a name was impossible for everyday use and was abbreviated first to the 'Third Foundation Dining Group' and then to just the 'Dining Group'.

We were not the only people, however, to be considering how to set up a new college for women in Cambridge. Very early we found that another group (which for the sake of simplicity I propose to call the 'New Hall Group') had already raised the question of a third women's undergraduate college with the then Vice-Chancellor, (Appendix II), but seemed not to have pursued the matter further. In Dr. Bidder's[7] view it was the existence of the Dining Group which had "galvanised them into activity, which is one of the important things that we did". Dame Rosemary Murray,[8] in her interesting

4 Between 1952 and 1965 there were 127 meetings of the Group. Though there were rarely more than 20 present at any one time, 52 women came at least 4 times. A detailed list of names and attendances is available in the College.

5 Advice given by Dr.J.T.Saunders who became Secretary General.

6 Sadly this restriction excluded at least one, Ethel Cruickshank, of the early and enthusiastic members. She was however convinced that the Regent House Principle was right and quietly withdrew.

7 Quotations from Dr. Anna Bidder come from her unpublished notes: "Unedited, unverified reminiscences . . . about the early days of the Dining Group.

8 Rosemary Murray was appointed Tutor in Charge of New Hall in 1953, became its first President in 1964 and remained in that office until her retirement in 1980.

history "New Hall 1954–1972, the making of a College", gives the date of the meeting with the Vice-Chancellor as December 1948. Shortly afterwards the New Hall Group called together a meeting where they invited 33 women whom they thought to be most interested. I and other members of the Dining Group well remember this meeting which was held in the drawing room of the Master's Lodge in Downing College.[9] Despite a small minority who held the surprising view that there were not enough able girls in the country to justify a new college and that to admit more to Cambridge "would only lead to a long tail of II(2) degrees", the majority did wish to see further facilities for the education of women in Cambridge.

After that meeting with the Vice-Chancellor at the end of 1948 there was an apparent lull in activity on the part of the University which continued for nearly four years. During the lull both groups, our Dining Group and the New Hall Group, continued independently to make plans. It later became apparent that in some ways the plans were similar: both thought that money for a new foundation should be sought outside the University, and that the college should start small and be based on an existing large house. It soon became apparent however that there was one fundamental difference. Whereas the plan of the New Hall Group involved collecting a number of students together and finding two or three senior members to look after them, our members believed it important to start with a strong academic nucleus, a good High Table, and to gather students round it. This view had considerable support in the University and here I quote again from Anna Bidder's reminiscences: "At this point I consulted the men I knew best in the University and said to each one, 'What is the most important thing to make a good College?', and they all replied, 'A good High Table'. This led to our concept of starting a women's undergraduate college by having a High Table of qualified women with a wide range of subjects ready as it were for the undergraduates when they came, and this was the principle to which we always adhered. The other group was largely concerned to make more places available for the very large number of women who were prevented from coming to Cambridge because of the restricted numbers in Newnham and Girton and they felt it more important to get something ready for them quickly than to have a strong academic nucleus. This was a continued difference of opinion as to policy between us, though the representatives of the two groups did frequently meet together.

The Dining Group's plan was in fact, as was pointed out by Dr. Wood-Legh, the way in which most of the older colleges had started. A group of scholars had settled together and drawn in pupils around them. This concept, which she later referred to as the 'Guild Principle', had been in the mind of Margaret Braithwaite ever since the day she had said, "We are the kind of people who could be used to make the nucleus of a new college." On that

9 Sir Lionel Whitby was then Master of Downing College. Lady Whitby presided at the meeting.

6

occasion she had amplified this remark by adding "because we are here and we are cheap because we do not need accomodation". In other words she, and the Dining Group, believed that both a sounder and more economic body could be made if the academic needs of the students could be supplied from a pool of senior M.A.s already resident in Cambridge, with their greatly varying research interests, rather than by the employment of two or three 'academic staff'.

Anna Bidder mentions that her father, Dr. G.P. Bidder, also a notable zoologist, had great sympathy with this project and wanted to make a capital gift so that the Dining Group could "put down a deposit for a house and so have real existence". This gift, made anonymously so as not to embarrass his daughter, was the subject of the earliest paper of the Dining Group that I can find. It is dated March 1951 and states: "When I learn of the existence of a bank account *on Trust to make a third foundation for women in connection with the University of Cambridge*, held by five Trustees who are women graduates of the University, I will then instruct my bankers to pay in two thousand pounds (£2,000) to that account as a gift for that Trust, without other condition. Donor Anonymous.[10] I would suggest for Trustees that three should be from your own group."

This handsome offer gave us great encouragement and we continued with our plans for a Third Foundation believing that we now had financial support. Unfortunately the fact that the terms of the offer were so wide led to some sad complications at a later date. However, by June, five Trustees[11] had been appointed and a Trust account opened at Barclays Bank.

About the time of the formation of this Trust, members of the Dining Group and of the New Hall Group, each still working independently, came together again in May 1951. Jointly they sent a letter to all women members of the Regent House asking if they "would be willing to give active support in the setting up of a New Foundation for women undergraduates". This information was important because it seemed that some members of the University, during the long period of waiting, were expressing doubts as to whether senior women already in the University were much interested in the idea. However, 90 out of the total of 110 women in the Regent House replied, and of these 75 said that they were keenly interested. Among the remainder, seven did not want any further provision made and the rest were not certain, but would not necessarily be in opposition. Further, the replies showed that among the senior members of the women's colleges some 75% were in favour of more women undergraduates in Cambridge. In October this information was sent to the Vice-Chancellor and to the Registrary in a letter signed by

10 In November 1954, some 10 months after his death, it became generally known that Dr.G.P.Bidder was the donor.
11 The Trustees of the George Bidder Fund were Anna Bidder, Margaret Braithwaite, Dorothy Needham, Helen Megaw and Barbara White.

two members of each group.[12] With this letter was sent a copy of a memorandum which had been prepared jointly earlier in the year and which carried about 20 signatures including members of both groups. This memorandum made suggestions as to how a new foundation could be constituted together with some notes on finance.

As time went on and we still waited for the University to recommend whether and how it proposed to make provision for more women students in Cambridge, the Dining Group was becoming better organised. In January 1951 we started to keep regular minutes of our meetings, so from here on it is possible to follow events with more precision. The minutes of the first seven months of that year show that the two groups were trying to work together to suggest how a new college for women could best be founded. A representative of each group accpted an invitation from the Vice-Chancellor to meet some University representatives to discuss the possibilities. This meeting was held on 31 January, when K. Wood-Legh represented the Dining Group.[13] The meeting was deemed generally to have been satisfactory in that the principle was accepted that a larger number of women students would be desirable. There had also been discussion on whether a new foundation should be collegiate or non-collegiate in character and on the proposals made in the memorandum which the two women's groups had submitted jointly. An additional paper had also been sent in by the Dining Group amplifying parts of the memorandum, and particularly pointing out our view that the body of women needed in a new foundation "might appropriately be drawn at first from the women members of the Regent House who were not Fellows of Girton or Newnham". It also maintained our belief that there was sufficient interest in the project for money to be forthcoming and supported this by saying that our own Trust had already reached almost £3,000.[14] No special mention was made of this paper at the meeting, but some doubts were expressed as to whether women not previously experienced would be capable of presenting students for matriculation.

Determined to be ready in time we in the Dining Group pressed on with our suggestions and plans. We estimated that £50,000 might be a suitable first target to meet the likely costs of a small foundation (see Appendix VII). We drew up a panel of possible teachers and appointed a committee to prepare a more detailed constitution than that in the memorandum already submitted. This committee was greatly helped by several senior members of the University, particularly by Professor S.J. Bailey, then Rouse Ball Professor of English Law. I well remember meetings in his rooms in St. John's College where, munching sandwiches, we thrashed out detailed proposals, amended them

12 The signatories were Anna Bidder and Dorothy Needham for the Dining Group.
13 Those present included Prof.Willink, Prof.Adcock, Dr.W.W.Grave, Prof.Fairlie, Miss Chrystal and the Heads of the Womens' Colleges.
14 An additional £1000 had come in from friends of Anna Bidder, including Penelope Jenkin, Mrs Richards & Geraldine Cadbury.

and gradually fitted them into a coherent whole. These became our 'Outline Proposals'.

Two months after the meeting arranged by the Vice-Chancellor we heard through the grapevine that the relevant University committee was to meet again shortly. This gave further stimulation and we sent a copy of our Outline Proposals, signed by 21 of our members, to the University, together with a financial statement. In mid-March 1952 we learned that the committee had decided that a new college of limited size for women was desirable. This naturally raised everyone's hopes that a new college could become a reality quite soon.

Anna Bidder, on behalf of the Dining Group, at once invited Dame Myra Curtis, then Principal of Newnham College and by now the most influential figure in the New Hall Group, to an informal meeting to discuss how the project could best be considered. The invitation was refused and the correspondence makes it sadly clear that there was still a divergence of view as to the most suitable way to proceed. In essence our Group wanted to go ahead straight away by calling a planning meeting of women members of the Regent House, a relatively small number, while the others wanted to wait till the University had approved the project and then to summon a "meeting of all senior women members of the University in Cambridge known to be interested".

Within the Dining Group itself discussion showed that there was now considerable variation of opinion. Some agreed with Dame Myra, but the majority were in favour of the view that a meeting of women members of the Regent House would be more effective than the very large meeting which she proposed. It was during this discussion that Margaret Braithwaite drew attention to a memorandum she had prepared, entitled 'The Third Foundation: analysis of points of difference between the two schools of thought' on how to form a new college. In this long, interesting if somewhat discursive analysis, she describes the two views as she saw them. One she describes as belonging to the 'Civil Service Principle' and the other to the 'Guild Principle'. By implication it was clear that she regarded the second to be the one held by the Dining Group and the first the one proposed by the other group. The Guild Principle has already been mentioned in connection with the Dining Group (see p.000). Sadly it is one that can too readily be misunderstood and mistaken for 'jobs for the girls'.

At last, in June 1952 (Reporter 1951/52, p.1395), the Council of the Senate published a report recommending that "a new autonomous foundation for women students should be set up with the restriction that the number of students should not, until further order, exceed one hundred". Next day the Dining Group received a letter from Dame Myra saying she now thought it "highly desirable" to summon a meeting, and that she was still of the same general opinion about what its composition should be. We agreed with this suggestion, although we feared that it might be unwise to hold such a large meeting before the University as a whole had formally discussed and approved the Council's recommendation. Nonetheless a joint committee was set up to organise a larger meeting.

Unfortunately, the original minutes of the next few meetings of the Dining Group are missing. However, by this time, typed copies of minutes of important meetings were circulated to all our members and such copies of two meetings in July and one in September are available. The July meetings were both concerned with the activities of the joint committee. Our representatives were Anna Bidder and Ena Mitchell, then Secretary of the Dining Group, and the meetings were minuted as having been "very cordial".

As the Registrary had advised that he did not think it wise at that juncture to plan too large a gathering, the committee decided that about 50 would be a suitable number. They agreed to ask Dame Myra to take the Chair at the meeting, which would be held on 30 July. In the end invitations were sent to 68 women[15] who were Fellows of Girton and Newnham, or members of the Dining Group, or those who had been concerned with the meeting with the Vice-Chancellor in January 1952.

After learning that the Registrary could see no objection to more than one scheme for starting a new college being put forward, we in the Dining Group again worked hard to prepare a revised version of our Outline Proposals. We hoped indeed that "the limited circulation of these would help to maintain the cordial feeling which had developed in the joint committee and make available for possible discussion the up-to-date thinking of the Dining Group". Unfortunately the proposals which had been revised "in the hope of meeting previous criticism and of removing ambiguities, had apparently aroused still more criticism". The main trouble apparently was that the idea of relying on women members of the Regent House for the first senior members included an element of self-selection which was felt by some to be objectionable. When this became known, the Dining Group decided at once to withdraw our Outline Proposals and no more, in that form, was ever heard of them.

The date duly arrived and the important meeting, planned by the joint committee, was held in the Women Graduates' Club in Mill Lane. Dame Myra was Chairman and the business ran smoothly, all nine resolutions put forward being passed nem. con. The most important of these was the establishment of an informal 'Association to Promote a Third Foundation for Women in the University of Cambridge'. Conditions of enrolment were approved and 40 members were enrolled then and there. A Chairman, Treasurer and Secretary were elected together with a committee of six.[16] The duties and powers of the committee were agreed and it was asked to start planning for fund-raising, to make enquiries about legal status, and about

15 The invitations had 8 signatories, 4 from each group.
16 Those elected were: Chairman. Mrs.Parsons; Secretary. Ena Mitchell; Treasurer. Barbara White; and the Committee included Anna Bidder and K.Wood-Legh for the Dining Group.

accommodation. It was an interim committee to be replaced by another as soon as the University gave its blessing to the project.

After this meeting, which really gave birth to New Hall, the Chairman of the Dining Group, then Anna Bidder, received, without warning, a memorandum from four of our members[17] suggesting that our Group should now be wound up since its aims had been overtaken by the Association for a Third Foundation now set up. In her reply Anna explained that she considered that the Group, in its meetings and its work together, had developed a coherence which could be valuable and should not be lost. These views were the main subject of prolonged discussions, spread over two meetings, which revealed a wide range of opinions. Some supported the idea that the Group should be abandoned at once for fear that we might be thought to be competing with the new association. Others suggested that we should turn ourselves into a dining club for social purposes only, while others agreed with the Chairman that something had been created which could still become useful. In the end Margaret Braithwaite suggested that we should adopt a policy of "masterly inactivity for the current term". This was gladly accepted by the majority and we agreed to postpone the question of disbandment for three months, to hold no business meetings during this period, and to abolish all committees. Sadly this decision led to the resignation of three valuable members[18] who all believed that immediate disbandment was the proper course. Thus the Dining Group remained quiescent, meeting only to dine and enjoy each other's company until February 1953.

During this quiescent period, important events were continuing elsewhere in connection with a new college for women. There was a University Discussion on the subject and only one person spoke, asking about student numbers. In answer it was pointed out that as the number of men undergraduates was expected to drop from 7,800 to 7,350 in 1956/7, the admission of an extra 100 women would not increase the total size of the student population. Since no vote was called for, there was no further delay and the recommendation was approved in November 1952 (Reporter 1952/3, p.460). So the University had finally given the signal that plans for the establishment of "a new autonomous foundation for women students" could really now go ahead.

Meetings of the new 'Third Foundation Association', formed in July 1952, were held during the winter and by February the members, men as well as women, numbered over 250. Elections were held and choice of officers and committee made. Although the new Secretary was a member of the Dining Group, no other member of that Group was elected to the committee which was a great disappointment. However, two men nominated by our Group were elected and gave valuable service to New Hall.[19] This election, in our

17 These were Margaret Keay, Inez Macdonald, Helena Shire and Edith Whetham.
18 These were Clare Fell, Inez Macdonald and Helena Shire.
19 These were Dr.David Thompson and Dr.Kitson Clark.

11

view, finally confirmed the fact that the Association in general wished the new college to develop along the lines favoured by Dame Myra, and that there was no place for the Dining Group in the venture. It was an unfortunate circumstance that in the voting the margins were narrow and some who came in late were, probably rightly, not allowed to vote. It so happened that the late members were all supporters of the Dining Group and this led to further sadness. However, the wish of the Association was accepted and the affairs of the new Third Foundation ceased to appear in the business of the Dining Group.

There were, however, two long-standing connections between the two bodies. One concerned the George Bidder Fund (see p.) and the other myself. As early as November 1953 one of the Trustees of the Fund wondered whether the money should be given to the new college since its aims seemed to fulfil the requirements of the rather vague terms of the Trust. Other Trustees were loath to hand over the money to an institution which was being funded in accordance with ideas very different from those which the original donor had wished to support. The other donors were consulted: one wished her gift to be given to New Hall and this was done in 1962; the others wanted the money to remain with the Trustees. Considerable correspondence took place, both parties accepting that both legal and moral issues were involved. Eventually it was mutually agreed that the money should belong to the Dining Group since by that time we had developed into the type of organisation more in accord with the views and ideas of the original donor.[20] Furthermore, it was recognised that, as New Hall had received some funds, what was a relatively small item to them was life-blood to us.

The other continuing connection with New Hall was that in October 1955 I was elected onto its first Council by the Association and was appointed Secretary of the Association itself. For 12 years I held this position and found it fascinatingly interesting. I learnt a great deal, not only about how an institution can be founded, but also about other colleges and their relation to the University. At Council meetings, where there were representatives of many colleges, whenever a subject came up for discussion, there was always someone who said "Well, the normal practice in a college is so and so". Immediately a chorus of other voices would strike up saying "Oh no, we never do that, we do so and so" and on it went. I learnt there how much variation exists between colleges and how complicated are the workings of the University. This was to prove invaluable in the future.

Others of the Dining Group also served New Hall at different times and in different ways and rejoiced to see it develop into a happy and successful college of the University. Further, to quote Anna Bidder, "the very fact that there was a third women's college changed the whole balance of the relationship between the men's and women's colleges since they became 'the Women's Colleges' instead of 'Newnham and Girton' ".

20 There is a summary of this correspondence in the College.

3. Development of the Dining Group

Before continuing the main story of the development of the Dining Group, let us look for a while at the domestic arrangements within the Group. For this we have again to search our memories, the 'dinner book', and the minute books, sources of different degrees of accuracy. Our memories are often vivid and definite, but do not always agree with one another. For example many of us remember with great precision an ornament which at one time always stood on the table at our dinners. All agreed that it had a palm tree with an animal standing underneath it. Most of us are certain they were in silver, but one stoutly maintains they were in brass. A majority remember clearly a camel under the palm, but some are convinced it was a horse and one knows it was an elephant!

The earliest 'dinner book' starts in the autumn of 1951 and shows that there were then about 25 people on the list and usually between 7 and 15 were dining each week. At first the Group was somewhat amorphous: the chairmanship rotated, there was no regular Secretary, no subscription and only ephemeral committees. The person who really gave cohesion was the Steward. This was K. Wood-Legh who indefatigably rang up every member every week in term-time to remind them of the dinner and to ask if they could come. She continued to do this until December 1954 when she became Chairman and was succeeded by Marian Clegg, Jay Evans and, in April 1960, by Eileen Clifford who held the post for nearly 20 years.

Perhaps this would be a suitable place to say a few words about K. Wood-Legh who died in October 1981. Though blind from early childhood, she was a notable scholar, publishing books on mediaeval church history which earned her a Litt.D. degree from Cambridge University and an invitation to give the highly respected Hulsean Lectures during 1970. She was a teacher with high academic standards who was determined from the start that the College should have students of its own and that the teaching and research should be of the best. To her friends she was even more remarkable for the way she dealt with lack of sight. She seemed to know who you were, even before you spoke, and she could remember exactly what had been said in an earlier paragraph when drafting, often suggesting a better alternative. Naturally she did not shine so much at meetings where people did not know her well, for difficulties in catching the Chairman's eye sometimes caused her to miss the opportunity of contributing to the discussion. She successfully arranged for a series of German girls to live with her, mostly university students, many of whom became her lasting friends. They were her eyes for her work and helping hands in her house and life. She made light of her affliction and liked it to be ignored. I believe that an episode which gave her very great pleasure was a day when someone outside the Dining Group was asking her if she could manage to get to a meeting. Anna Bidder overheard and said "Oh, she will manage it all right, we never worry about K." My family used to be amused when we gave parties in our garden ten miles outside Cambridge, for it seemed that it was the male undergraduates who rang up to ask how to get there, the girls who bicycled and K. Wood-Legh who walked.

We were, in the early days, a peripatetic group. After the first lunches in a Trinity Street restaurant, we dined in a variety of places before settling down to a spell of over three years at the Copper Kettle in Kings Parade. Here the kindly manageress was able to give us a room to ourselves. Here also was the much remembered metal ornament. Previously we had met in another cafe in Kings Parade, which was pleasant but without privacy, in the restaurant of the Victoria Cinema, which was vast, empty and daunting, and in the Women Graduates' Club, which, in the evenings, was dark, cold and discouraging. Anna Bidder remembers, "It was at one of our dinners at the Victoria Cinema that Marian Clegg came for the first time and she and Margaret Braithwaite got into passionate talk on the Chinese language, one a geographer, the other a moral scientist . . . As we came away from that dinner, thinking about that conversation, I said to myself: 'we are now a college'." Those dinners, and the meetings which often followed them, were immensely stimulating and great fun. We were all inspired by a common aim, but while waiting to fulfil it, were also greatly enjoying the kind of companionship that others gained in their colleges. We always hoped that in some way this ebullient nucleus could be of use to the new undergraduate women's college we hoped to establish or help to etablish. Then, as mentioned above, came the disappointment that, as a Group, we were no longer to be involved in the new venture that we had planned so diligently.

During the quiescent period, after the birth of the Third Foundation Association, we continued to dine at the Copper Kettle as before and went on doing so until the summer of 1955, when the management there found that they could no longer let us have a separate room. This prompted a move to the West House Hotel in West Road where we met together happily for the next eight years. As time went on the volume of business increased and in order to speed up meetings, I remember little groups leaving the room to discuss resolutions and amendments on the stairs, much to the surprise of the other visitors in the hotel. So it was probably as well that the Master of Gonville and Caius College, then Dr. Joseph Needham, in his kindness, invited us in 1963 to hold our dinners in their new hostel, Harvey Court, also in West Road. Here, in a pleasant small dining hall which we had to ourselves, and with a generous subsidy from that College, we continued to dine. This move was felt to be an important landmark as we were then able to meet regularly within a College rather than in a hotel or restaurant. Accordingly we now wore gowns as is traditional in Cambridge Colleges.

Not only was our Constitution amorphous at the start, but so also were the finances of the Group. In Anna Bidder's words, "We had no regular

14

subscription, people used to pay as and when they felt flush. We made it a rule that nobody should be prevented from joining the Dining Group because they could not afford to come. Some people could give regular attendance, some people could give money, and we never found any difficulty in financing ourselves under these conditions, and indeed, when the policy changed and the regular subscription began, we had saved £200 if I remember rightly." This system worked well until the size of the Group increased and guest nights were introduced. The subscription, when it came, covered items such as hire of room, guests and postage, while we paid for our own food and drink.

Guest nights were important and from the very early days we entertained, in addition to personal guests, those who had helped the Group or who might otherwise be interested in our activities[21]. In fact our first corporate possession was a fine Visitors' Book. It was presented in January 1955 by Etheljohn Lindgren,[22] one of our earliest members, and has been in use ever since. One of the early social highlights of the Group was a dinner in the summer of 1954 when we had the wines of three George Bidder's on the table. Anna writes: "We had a sherry that had been laid down by my great grandfather, we had clarets laid down by my grandfather and clarets laid down by my father."

We also started to offer hospitality to academic women visiting Cambridge from other countries, both those invited by the University and the academic wives of the University's male guests. Such women otherwise often felt somewhat neglected as at that time the men's colleges could not entertain women in their dining halls, while Newnham and Girton really had no space and were therefore unable to offer regular dining privileges. So we were able to help both the University and ourselves by giving dining rights to these visitors who certainly added much to our interest and enjoyment.

Throughout the history of the Dining Group we were careful to keep a close scrutiny on the official journal, the University Reporter, to watch for names of new women admitted to the Regent House and to ensure that each of these knew of the Group's existence and was given the opportunity to join if she wished, provided that she was not already a Fellow of another college. As time went on we became increasingly conscious of the activities, reports and discussions taking place in the University. As Anna says we became "more actively aware of the University as a body towards which we had individual and corporate responsibilities. I think that this was one of the most important fruits of those early days". At the same time we realised that for the Group to be effective we must maintain as high an academic standard as possible. This in itself gave "a sense of responsibility that it was important

21 Our first guests were Professor Bailey and Dr.J.T.Saunders.
22 She always maintained that Glyn Daniel's account in his autobiography, "Some Small Harvest" of her tenure of a lectureship in the Department of Archaeology was inaccurate in several important respects.

to try and get work published because of its help for the reputation of the Group". As one who, because of domestic cares, had been working part-time and with no real connection with any colleges, she adds, "Here at last was a group who cared whether one was working or not and this, as far as I was concerned, made the most enormous difference."

4. Concern for Graduates

The Third Foundation Association was actively creating the college which was going to become New Hall, when the Dining Group began to hold business meetings again. The lull of four months had allowed us all to get used to the idea that we were not after all going to found another undergraduate college for women, and that we had now to start again with open minds as to what the future should hold for us. Certainly not then, nor at any time, did we wish to be only a social dining club.

At this point it would be well to look and see what else was happening in the University as a whole. Steps were widely being taken to cope with the larger undergraduate numbers. Two new colleges, Churchill as well as New Hall, were about to be founded, Fitzwilliam House was turning itself from a non-collegiate to a collegiate institution on a new site, and many of the other colleges were adding to their buildings. In fact probably the 1950s and 1960s saw more college building than at any time in the history of the University.[23] Accommodation was at a premium and the pressure was accentuated by the fact that many Cambridge landladies, who had formerly housed undergraduates, learned during the war, when regional government increased, that other tenants were more profitable. Undergraduates were only in Cambridge for about half the year while Government servants, for example, were there for the full 52 weeks (Appendix III).

Attention was now turning also to graduates, both research students and particularly to senior members. With the expansion of the University after the war and especially the growth of the science departments, the number of senior members involved in teaching and research increased rapidly. Those who were Fellows had full benefit of collegiate life, but those for whom there was no place in a college were relatively left out in the cold. They were to some extent second class citizens and their plight later became known as the 'non-Fellow problem'.

As early as December 1947 the University had considered the establishment of a Faculty Club. At that time as many as 400 of the 900 members of the Regent House had little or no connection with a college. This state of affairs was recognised as unfortunate, and as a remedy the creation of an institution

23 Reference. "The Colleges of Cambridge" by Bryan Little an "Adams and Dart".1973.

"which would help to promote the social integration of all seniors who serve the University" was recommended (Reporter 1947/48, p.349). On several occasions there were discussions about possible sites and premises for such an institution and there was even a syndicate set up to decide whether or not women were to be included since they already had a Graduates' Club of their own. In the event, the name 'Faculty Club' was dropped and in October 1950 the 'University Combination Room' materialised in the beautiful room in the Old Schools which had been the Catalogue Room of the University Library before it was moved in 1934 to its present site in Grange Road. This Combination Room is open to all members of the Regent House of both sexes and it has been a delightful and valuable addition to University life. But it did not remove the need for more care for those who did not fully belong to any of the colleges.

This then was the scene when Margaret Braithwaite, usually the one among us with the greatest foresight, sent an Open Letter in February 1953 to all members of the Dining Group "containing suggestions for a five-year policy". The gist of her plan was a recommendation to build up the Dining Group intellectually, socially and financially, so that by slow growth it could develop into a Regent House women's guild. There was to be no immediate thought of turning into a college, but she added that she could not quite give up the hope that, in the very long run, such a guild might develop "collegiate potentialities". In proposing that we should at once start collecting money, she stressed that "care must of course be taken . . . that the Dining Club draws funds only from sources not available to the Third Foundation Association". Money was needed for premises, for hospitality and for grants. These grants were particularly to help "Cambridge academic women with family responsibilities who might qualify for membership (of the Regent House) if they could be freed a little from home ties".

We, in the Dining Group, gladly accepted these ideas and at once set to work to consider how they could be put into practice. We were already exploring the possibility of getting permission to use the Hall of Pythagoras for our dinners and meetings. This handsome 12th century building, then belonging to Merton College, Oxford, was at that time lying empty. Questions and discussions on this subject occurred frequently during the next two years, but eventually the scheme was shown to be impracticable.[24] Later St. John's College acquired the building, restored it at great expense, and it now forms an integral and valuable part of that College.

Policy discussions also continued actively and all members agreed that before the Group could become more permanent, it must be strengthened and its Constitution crystallised, despite strong feelings that its happy informality should not be lost. As a result the Group's officers were asked to take a more active part and in October 1954 they were requested to consider

24 Correspondence between Anna Bidder and Lord Rothschild.

"the conditions necessary for the Dining Group to consolidate itself so that it can obtain University support, and become a money-raising body". The recommendations of the officers were put forward under three headings. The first concerned the structure of the Group itself, including a proposal for a simple form of Constitution. This defined the 'Purpose and Aims' in the following words: "the fundamental purpose (of the Group) is to have concern for the problems of academic women in Cambridge and, by providing practical assistance and the stimulus of regular social contact, to encourage academic achievement in teaching, learning and research". The Constitution also suggested a detailed procedure for the election of officers, for their tenure, for regulating financial affairs and for arranging business meetings. In general the main suggestions were accepted. The elections became more formal and the officers tended to hold office for longer periods, though re-elected annually: for example K. Wood-Legh became Chairman and carried out the duties with skill and efficiency for nearly eight years before she was succeeded by Anna Bidder.

The second heading in the officers' recommendations concerned 'Gaining University Support'. The first step here should be to make known our activities and aims to a number of influential senior members of the University and try to secure their co-operation. Seeking the advice and views of such people was usually done at dinner, and our guest lists of that time include many names of those experienced in both University and college affairs. We had already been much encouraged by the Secretary General, then Dr. J.T. Saunders, who, in a personal letter to Anna Bidder said, "I very much hope that you will go ahead with your plans for the Group because there is undoubtedly a need for such an association of persons who are not Fellows of colleges and this association could be formed most easily among the women where the numbers are smaller and easier to handle." Another view[25] was that the Group was too small to get University support and that we should join with the large number of men in the same non-collegiate condition. After much discussion our general feeling was that such a large group would not answer the problems of the non-collegiate people, that the present Group would lose its feeling of being an entity, and that the interests of the women would be swamped. So we continued alone, and I think it fair to say that almost everyone we approached was both interested in our ideas and gave us encouragement.

The third and last of the officers' suggestions was connected with 'Money Raising'. It stressed the importance of seeking funds in order to get premises and to give us "capital backing as a first step towards obtaining University recognition".

In October 1954, when I was involved in both the Dining Group and the newly-opened New Hall, I received a long and interesting letter from Margaret

25 View put forward by Prof.Arberry of King's College.

Braithwaite suggesting ways in which the relations between the two organisations could become closer. Her main suggestion was that the Dining Group could be an integral part of the new college providing a ready-made academic nucleus. She considered that such an arrangement could be regarded as analogous with the relationship between King's College and its Choir School where a smaller part of an organisation provides a service to the larger. I do not remember any discussion of this letter and as no mention of it appears in the minutes, I presume that the matter went no further. However, there was a happy link with New Hall in that its Tutors[26] dined occasionally with the Dining Group when they could leave their own emerging institution.

5.   The Non-Fellow Problem

After streamlining our organisation, our activities in seeking support from people who might like to help us continued increasingly. Increasing also was the concern within the University for those without a college. A Discussion on the subject, under the title of 'A Topic of Concern for the University' had been held in the Senate House as early as February 1955 (Reporter 1954/5, p.758 and 945). I was there, listening to the many speeches which showed the general view to be that somehow such people should become affiliated with existing colleges, but no definite plans were made. Shortly afterwards our President, formerly known as Chairman, met the Vice-Chancellor and suggested to him that the activities of our Group might indicate another possible solution to the problem. He was said to be very much interested in our ideas and thought that we could become a pilot project. He therefore suggested that we should draw up a memorandum to explain to the Council of the Senate what we were doing and hoping to do.

The preparation of this memorandum was our next main task. The drafting was mainly done by the President, Kathleen Wood-Legh, and Anna Bidder, but it was much discussed by the Group and shown to the chief officers of the University as well as to other kind advisers. Finally the amended and polished version, headed 'Memorandum Submitted by the Society of Women Members of the Regent House who are not Fellows of Colleges (the 'Dining Group')', was sent to the Council of the Senate at the end of May 1955. It gave an account of the history, structure and activities of the Group and its relevance to the non-Fellow problem. The introduction included the belief that "it is unreasonable to expect the existing colleges to remedy this condition (the non-Fellow problem); since to increase their senior membership sufficiently to meet the need would not only cause grave material difficulties, but would create bodies so large that they would lose their essential quality. It seems, therefore, that experiments in new forms of group life by members

26 The first Tutors were Rosemary Murray and Hope Hammond.

of the Regent House who are not Fellows of a college may at this time be of interest and value. It is for this reason that the experience and problems of a group engaged in such an experiment are laid before the Council of the Senate in this memorandum".

The memorandum then went on to ask if the University could be persuaded to give the Dining Group some sort of status within the University. This was needed in order that we could progress from being an informal society to incorporation as a legal entity able to hold funds and be registered as a charity. We appreciated that there was difficulty in that its Statutes at that time allowed the University only to grant recognition to institutions which were educating students reading for Cambridge degrees. We therefore suggested that our problem, or the problem of similar groups in the future, "might best be met could some basis of University recognition be found, suitable for groups with no attached body of undergraduates". Further, we thought that the work of such groups in "stimulating the research work and academic life of their members and in assisting the educational work of the University" could be regarded as a suitable basis.

In a long and friendly reply the Registrary[27] said that the Council of the Senate "were much interested to hear of the activities of the Group", welcomed its "attempt to satisfy a real need" and "congratulated its members both on their initiative and on their success". However, he explained that the Council could see no prospect that the University would be prepared in the forseeable future, so soon after the start of New Hall, to recognise another institution for women even if its student membership were restricted to graduate research students. Also the Council considered that there was not yet enough evidence to warrant asking for a change to be made in the University Statutes so that new kinds of institutions could be recognised. The letter ended "for the reasons given above the Council feel unable to sponsor development of the Group on the lines suggested in the Memorandum, but they hope, and in view of what has already been achieved, they are confident, that the Group will continue to flourish and to fulfil a useful function pending the emergence of a Faculty Club with which it might possibly be associated or the establishment at some later date of a more general case for widening the class of institution which could be formally recognised by the University".

So, our first attempt to gain official recognition by the University had failed. It was almost exactly ten years later, in June 1965, that we sent in our third, and this time successful, application. The second unsuccessful one was in 1963 (see p.). I am interested to see that, concerning the first application, Anna Bidder noted, "This was not wholly wise in its formulation since we were so rash as to liken ourselves to a sort of Cambridge All Souls and this was regarded as the mouse comparing itself to the mountain!"

Once again we had to think anew about what to do next. In fact the next

27 The Registrary then was Mr.R.M.Rattenbury.

four years, 1956–60, turned out to be for us a period of relative inactivity. We continued to dine together regularly and to go on with our normal recruitment procedure. We also invited many who were active in University affairs to dinners, guest nights and other social occasions. These were all opportunities to make more widely known our ideas and activities and to ask advice and views on how a group like ours might progress.

Business meetings were less frequent, but two important proposals appeared. The first was the suggestion that the Group should add to its membership as 'Associates' some women who were not in the Regent House. At first sight this was an attractive idea as the presence of a wider range of people at our dinners would give added interest and support. However, it was soon realised that the inclusion of such members would alter the character of the Group as we had described it to the Council of the Senate. After lengthy discussion we agreed to adhere to the structure we had shown in our memorandum and so the proposal to add an extra category to our membership was reluctantly postponed. The second new proposal was that a Capital Fund should be started. Margaret Braithwaite suggested that such a fund, if it could be used "to assist senior academic work", might make it easier for us to become registered as a charity. A short memorandum was circulated to all members and the discussion which followed showed that a few thought we were not yet sufficiently stable to become a charity, but the majority approved of the scheme and said they would be prepared to covenant for it. Nevertheless, no action was taken before the Group became involved in the general movements in the University in connection with non-Fellows.

After the long Senate Discussion, already mentioned, in February 1955, there was no outward sign of any resultant activities within the University for over two years. In October 1957 an article by Mr. L.P. Wilkinson of King's College was published in the 'Cambridge Review'[28] saying " . . . it can be strongly argued that the chief need of Cambridge at present is not to found colleges of the traditional type, which will simply increase the strain on the capacity of the University, not to mention the city, but to provide a home for those members of the Regent House who cannot be absorbed in the governing bodies of the existing colleges". Referring to this article, our President, K. Wood-Legh, and Secretary, Nora Willson, wrote jointly to the Review a letter describing the activities of the Dining Group, then 31 in number, and explaining how it was helping "to provide some of the amenities of a collegiate society for those women members of the Regent House who are not Fellows of a college". Then in December 1957 the Council of the Senate put forward another recommendation that a 'University Club' should be established. After much discussion, a further report and two questionnaires, it was generally agreed that such a club was needed and plans for setting it

28 The relevant references to the Cambridge Review are: L.P.Wilkinson. Bulges and Colleges,19.10.1957, p.40. Letter from K Wood-Legh & Nora Willson,9.11.1957, p.141. C.A.Talyst. St.Mary's College. 10.10.1959, p.5.

up were made accordingly. This was followed in October 1959 by the new idea that a graduate college for both sexes should be founded, possibly to be called 'St. Mary's College'. In fact neither of these proposals materialised because by 1960 the University had come to the conclusion that the whole question of "the relationship between the University and the colleges" needed reconsideration.

The means chosen for the study of this relationship was to set up a Syndicate, ask it to make a wide survey and to make recommendations. The Syndicate consisted of 14 members, three of whom were from other universities (Oxford and Leicester), and the Chairman was Lord Bridges.[29] As only one woman, the Principal of Newnham, then Ruth Cohen, had been appointed, we in the Dining Group and 12 others, mostly men who supported us, wrote to the Registrary asking for an additional woman to represent the "women graduate staff who are not Fellows of colleges". However, disappointingly, no further appointments were made to the Syndicate itself, but some of our members and other women served on their committees.

Cambridge was not alone in having a large number of non-Fellows for the problem was acute also in Oxford where in 1962 there were said to be as many as 250 non-Fellows to 504 Fellows.[30]

As soon as they started work the Syndicate invited memoranda from both institutions and individuals. The Dining Group decided at once to accept the invitation and, as memoranda had to be submitted by the end of the year, 1960, great activity was generated. Extra business meetings discussed a series of drafts produced by a new drafting committee. Finally on 29 December the President was able to send to the Syndicate 30 copies of our document, together with short notes on our members.

The memorandum stated that we fully agreed that an urgent need existed in the University for a centre where men and women would meet on an equal footing and where the officers of the University and of the colleges could all belong on equal terms. However, our main concern was to point out "the advantages to be gained from an extension of the collegiate system". In addition to the traditional colleges we believed there was room for small · new collegiate societies whose members would be mainly drawn from the non-Fellows of the University. If these members carried "the rights and duties with regard to University administration that now fall to the Fellows (of existing colleges), the present unsatisfactory division (between Fellows and non-Fellows) would largely disappear". We recognised that fellowship of a college involved "a full weight of responsibility and sheer hard work" and was "not a matter of status and privilege alone". We mentioned the history and activities of our own group and our belief that small societies did not

29 As Sir Edward Bridges he was Permanent Secretary to the Treasury from 1945 until 1956 when he retired.
30 Reference Cambridge Review. Basil Mitchell. "The position of Non-Fellows at Oxford." 28.4.1962. p.378.

require great wealth for their establishment and could be set up quickly. We ended by stressing that the University needed "pioneers as well as traditionalists among its corporate as among its individual members".

For nearly one and a half years the Syndicate amassed facts and deliberated and we eagerly awaited their findings. During this period of waiting the Dining Group quietly continued to spread its ideas and to consolidate itself. We began collecting together a group of senior men into a consultative body to advise us and some of its members later became our first Trustees. We asked for and obtained permission to hold a business meeting in a University lecture room to show that we felt ourselves nearly a University body. We had earlier also asked if we could put a notice in the unofficial part of the 'University Reporter', but were gently refused on the grounds that at that time we were a social and not an academic body. We took a particular interest in the elections to the Council of the Senate, supporting those we knew to be sympathetic to our aims and, to our great satisfaction, one of our members, Dr. Barbara Reynolds[31], then a University Lecturer in Italian, was elected. Within our Group the election of officers was again postponed until after the Syndicate reported. Also during this period, Anna Bidder, then our Financial Secretary, had sabbatical leave and was away in the Pacific studying the Pearly Nautilus, that fascinating mollusc whose shell adorns the college crest today. I too, from January to March 1962, was away in the then British Guiana studying Manatees (Sea-cows).

In May 1961 the Dining Group was invited to send a representative to a meeting of the Syndicate and it was agreed that the President, K. Wood-Legh, should attend. She decided not to take a written statement with her, but to discuss beforehand with the Group and other supporters, what questions were likely to be asked and the line which her answers might take. The interview itself turned out to be largely a matter of clarifying points in our memorandum.

Eventually in March 1962 the findings of the Bridges Syndicate were published (Reporter 1961/2, p.1075). The report was massive, covering many aspects of University and college life, and the recommendations were far-reaching. Insofar as they concerned the non-Fellow problem, their gist was that a schedule should be drawn up of 'qualified officers' (i.e. those without fellowship or membership of a college), that each existing college should admit a quota of these and that financial assistance should be available to enable them to do so. Also the urgent need for a University Centre was stressed and possibly also for a Graduate College. The Council of the Senate then took the unusual step of inviting written memoranda and comments on the Syndicate's report before a general Discussion to be held on 22.5.62.

31 Barbara Reynolds was the first of our members to be elected to the Council of the Senate and was followed by Mary Hesse in 1963, Kate Bertram in 1973 and Phyllis Bowden in 1983. Dr.Reynolds left Cambridge to become Warden of Willoughby Hall (1963/9), then Reader in Italian studies (1969/75), in Nottingham University.

These were published, including one from our Group. This one of ours, largely drafted by Margaret Braithwaite, was a fine provocative but persuasive document which, according to Anna, was received with very considerable surprise and interest by the University. Three years later it was specially mentioned in a report of the Council of the Senate. It started with a preamble which said, "The cut, on a national basis, in the expected University grant has made the Bridges Syndicate Report out of date within a few days of its publication. The fact that it dealt explicitly with a past situation and did not look forward sufficiently to future developments, has meant that it has all the more easily and quickly become archaic. It now remains to be seen whether we can save the basic recommendation of the report, namely the continuation of a collegiate structure for Cambridge, if we adopt a more flexible conception of a college." The assumption of the Syndicate that Cambridge could remain fully collegiate was also questioned in a leading article in the Cambridge Review.[32]

Our memorandum then went on to propose that the University encourage "unofficial new groups which, starting spontaneously in order to render some service to the University, or to the nation, or both, gain a connection with the University such that they develop into colleges". These collegiate groups should function in areas not covered by the existing colleges which were largely concerned with undergraduates. There were "many urgent needs: care of research students, care of graduates from overseas, provision for men and women, graduates and undergraduates, returning to academic life after some break in their careers, needs of Commonwealth students, of research workers, and of the increasing flood of academic visitors of all kinds, who come to Cambridge for varying lengths of time. Perhaps the greatest need of all is to encourage, and provide better conditions for the freelance supervisors, upon whose skill, time and devotion the University daily depends".

Another major point made in the memorandum was that the large sums of money generally believed to be necessary to start a college would not be needed because collegiate societies could begin in a small way. Only when they had proved themselves would they be justified in appealing for the capital required for expansion. However, since "the early years of a small growing enterprise depend, even more than those of a larger group, on the qualities of its Head" the University might be asked to help by guaranteeing an initial salary. This should be sufficient to justify asking someone of exceptional suitability and distinction to devote the whole of her or his time to the development of the new group. In conclusion, the memorandum states that "the collegiate scheme here put forward proposes an alternative solution to the non-Fellow problem to that of the Syndicate's report" and then summarises its advantages[33] (Reporter 1961/62, p1733).

32 Reference the leading article in Cambridge Review entitled "What tunes for the Piper." 28.4.62. p.377.
33 Apart from this joint effort, two of our members sent in individual comments: Anna Bidder (p.1742) and Mary Hesse (p/1744).

24

While the University was digesting the report of the Bridges Syndicate and the comments made upon it, let us consider some of the people mentioned in our memorandum as needing special care. First there were the research students who were increasing rapidly in numbers each year. These were all attached to the various colleges, but at that time the colleges were really geared to a two-tier system of Fellows and undergraduates. The research students lay between and although special common rooms were made available for them, these students, especially if they were from overseas, often felt somewhat neglected. A University Centre would help them, but would not provide a complete solution to their problems. Already one college, Corpus Christi, had set up on its land a special residential block of rooms at Leckhampton House solely for its research students.

Academic visitors also sometimes felt that they were missing an important part of Cambridge life as they were not necessarily connected with any college. The problem was more acute with women for their hosts were at that time not yet able to take them to dine in their colleges and would have to entertain them outside the University. Happily, as mentioned above, we in the Dining Group were already helping the University by offering hospitality to such women who, as much as we, enjoyed the arrangement.

As for people wishing to return to academic work after a gap, we were making known how our group was aiming "to explore, and to contribute to the solution of, the national problem of bringing back to academic life older women for whom family or other claims have made an interruption in their careers".

The situation for many supervisors was highly unsatisfactory. In Cambridge the colleges as well as the University take part in the education of the undergraduates. The University is responsible for the formal teaching, the lectures, the laboratories and the arrangement of examinations, while the colleges provide the 'supervision', the teaching in small groups which is felt to be such an important part of the Cambridge system. The larger colleges with their large fellowship can usually find a high proportion of their supervisors from within their own college. With increasing specialisation in most subjects, however, the numbers of supervisors needed rises rapidly and individuals are often asked to teach in many colleges. Increasingly in the early 1960s, academic women, often wives of University Lecturers, were teaching in both women's and men's colleges. The normal practice is for a college to give dining privileges, or some form of membership, to its supervisors who thus come to know the other people concerned with the undergraduates they are teaching. But if the supervisor for a man's college was a woman there was then no opportunity for her to meet with the other teachers or for feed-back from those employing her.

It was while waiting for the University's reaction to the Bridges Report that Anna Bidder, newly-returned from the Pacific, brought to the Dining Group an idea which turned out to be one of major importance. This was that we, as a Group, should invite to dinner any of the women supervising for the men's colleges who would like to come and who had no real connection with a college. The idea was welcomed and Margaret Braithwaite undertook to guarantee financial backing for this hospitality for a term. A letter from the Group was then sent to the Heads of all colleges explaining our offer and asking them to give us the names of their women supervisors. The answers, often with friendly good wishes, provided a long list of names. After deducting those who had died, gone to Manchester or become a college Fellow, we were left with 27 names. To each of these we sent an invitation to a dinner with the following explanation: "We are asking you to dinner as a supervisor for a man's college and therefore without dining rights in the college where you supervise, and would be glad if you could join us on this occasion. We are hoping, by degrees, to make contact with all the women supervisors from the men's colleges." The first dinner for them was held at the end of November 1962 when 10 dined with us. The dinners were an instant success and Anna describes how "there was not a woman in the room who was not immediately in eager and active conversation. They were thirsty for it and they very much welcomed the opportunity to talk with us and we very much welcomed the stimulus and pleasure which their presence gave us". The dinners continued and some of those early supervisers later became our own Fellows and Senior Members.

The possibility of admitting to membership of the Group men who had no connection with a college was also discussed and at least one member made it clear that she would prefer to support a mixed, rather than a single-sex, society.[34] While expressing sympathy with this point of view, the Group agreed that as the University at that time contained only single-sex institutions, we would be wise to proceed on the lines most likely to gain immediate recognition.

After the publication in March 1962 of the report of the Bridges Syndicate, the Council of the Senate published its recommendations in July of that year (Reporter 1961/2, p.2122). The two most important proposals, from the point of view of the Dining Group, were that a University Centre should be established straight away and that a committee should be set up to investigate the possibilities of starting graduate colleges or other societies for graduates.

Everyone appeared to be in favour of a University Centre; its plans, construction and development went steadily ahead and it was finally opened in November 1967 by Sir Isaac Wolfson, its main benefactor. It provides an excellent meeting place for all senior members of the University, research students, mature undergraduates and their spouses. Like the University Combination Room earlier, it is a very valuable asset, but not a full answer to the non-Fellow problem.

---

34 Mary Hesse, who later became so much involved in setting up University College that she decided to leave Lucy Cavendish and become one of the first Fellows of the new College.

The investigation into the possible introduction of graduate institutions was carried out by a committee of the Council of the Senate[35] consisting of six senior men and our Barbara Reynolds, who, as already mentioned, (see p.) was then a member of the Council. This committee, on a number of occasions, met a Sub-Committee set up by the colleges which included Anna Bidder, who was welcomed as a person very knowledgeable on the subject. As a result of its studies the committee recommended that a change be made in the Statutes of the University so that the proposed new 'collegiate societies' could be formally recognised. It also suggested that such societies might need University help in the way of accommodation and finance to enable them to emerge. Written comments were again invited, discussions held and interim reports published.

Meanwhile there were some changes within the Dining Group. At the start of 1963 Anna Bidder became our President and remained in that office for two years. Then she became the first President of the official society when we were recognised as part of the University in 1965. The need for a new office of Vice-President was recognised and Kathleen Wood-Legh and Margaret Braithwaite were jointly elected. The elections for the other officers, postponed for so long because of the wait for the report of the Bridges Syndicate, were also held. These put me into the secretaryship[36] where I stayed until I became the first Tutor after recognition two years later. The Treasurer and Steward Nora Willson and Eileen Clifford, originally elected in 1958 and 1959, respectively were both re-elected and continued in office well into our official existence.

6. Societies for Graduates

In June 1963 the Council's report on 'Societies for Graduates' was published (Reporter 1962/63, p.1793), including the statement that "the Council's view is that the existence of new collegiate societies of the kinds envisaged by the committee will be in the interests of the University . . . ". It also agreed to consider the amendment of Statute H of the University, and to bear in mind the needs of such societies in connection with property, but reserved its view as to whether University money could be used.

Interestingly, in the same number of the Reporter, the Council also made known that it had already received a letter from Caius, St. John's and Trinity

35 The Council of the Senate took the unusual step of publishing the names of those appointed. These were Sir Eric Ashby, Mr.J.S.Boys Smith, Mr.K.E..Berrill, Mr.W.A.Camps, Professor D.L.Page, and Dr.Barbara Reynolds with the Vice Chancellor as Chairman. The Sub-committee appointed by a committee of representatives of the Colleges consisted of Dr.A.M. Bidder, Mr.W.A.Camps, Mr.T.C.Thomas, Dr David Thompson and Dr.M.G.Young.
36 End of handwritten minutes.

Colleges saying that they had together agreed to establish a "new college society for graduates" to be called 'Darwin College' (Reporter 1962/3, p.1734). Two months later the Council itself set up a committee to consider the establishment of a 'University College' (Reporter 1963/4, p.1120), though neither scheme could come into effect without changes in University Statutes. (Appendix IV.)

Directly the Council's report appeared, the Dining Group prepared an application for recognition as a collegiate society. This, signed by the President and the two Vice-Presidents, was finally sent off to the Council on 29.7.63. The application described the activities of the Group and the two categories of women with whom we would be mainly concerned, namely women supervising or doing distinguished academic work for the colleges; and a body of graduate and research students. It also stressed that we could help with the problem of enabling older women to return to professional life. The need for premises was mentioned as well as the fact that we were taking steps towards becoming a legal charity. We made it clear that we were not "asking for any direct financial assistance from the University", but would appreciate help in obtaining suitable premises and possibly a guarantee for the salary of a Head for a few years. We had always envisaged a Head from outside our number, hence the plea for a stipend. Financially we had till then been self-supporting, had a capital sum of £1,500-£2,000 and aimed to raise as soon as possible an initial sum of £20,000 to £25,000, (see inflation table in Appendix VII).

In his reply, dated 2.8.63, the Registrary said that the Council "expressed sympathy with the society's intentions, but could not take any action under the existing provisions of Statute H". Furthermore, he explained that until the Group had accommodation and was constituted as a legal charity, it could not be considered for University recognition.

So ended our second application to the University for recognition. The reply was accepted philosophically, especially as the Vice-Chancellor, then Sir Ivor Jennings, in his retiring Address two months later, stated that a proposal "to found a Graduate Women's College, at present unnamed, is under consideration". Clearly our next step should be to find premises and press forward with our moves for incorporation as a Trust so as to be ready to take advantage of any amendment to Statute H which the University might consider.

For incorporation both Trustees and a Trust Deed were needed. Although the Group had been considering a Trust Deed since August 1962 when the first draft was prepared for us,[37] it was a year later before actual steps were taken to find Trustees. Naturally, the first three people to be suggested were the 'triumvirate', who had started the Group. However, the importance of having some outside people was felt from the beginning. Though records are

37 The solicitor concerned was Mr.Alfred Braithwaite of Waterhouse Co. of Lincoln's Inn.

scarce, it seems that K. Wood-Legh first asked Bishop Chase, a friend and neighbour, if he would become a Trustee. He was formerly Bishop of Ripon and Master of Selwyn College and a most wise, experienced and kindly man. It was he who advised that we should have eight Trustees, four internal and four external. Then Anna Bidder, coming out of the Friends Meeting House one Sunday morning, took the opportunity of inviting Sir Joseph Hutchinson to join us. "Gladly, Anna, gladly," was his reply. He was then Draper's Professor of Agriculture and a man who strongly wished to expand the scope of women's education in Cambridge.

About the same time Margaret Braithwaite successfully drew Professor Noel Annan, then Provost of King's College,[38] into the trusteeship. Then came a disappointment for it was found legally impossible for a blind person to be a Trustee. K. Wood-Legh therefore sadly had to withdraw and Margaret Bottrall, then Tutor of Hughes Hall, was asked to take her place. She had been active, together with K. Wood-Legh and Valerie Joysey, in the Group in connection with constitution-making and had also been concerned with the new constitution of Hughes Hall. The fourth internal Trustee was Nora Willson who was then Treasurer of the Dining Group and Senior Lecturer in Homerton College. The fourth external Trustee was Mr. W.A. Camps, then Master of Pembroke College, who had served with Anna Bidder on a Committee when the Council of the Senate were investigating the possibility of graduate institutions.

There was much discussion at all stages of the growth of the Trust Deed and drafts passed backwards and forwards between the Trustees, the Dining Group and the legal advisers. In the end it was agreed that the objects of the Trust were to enable the Group to be "responsible for the care and discipline of: a) research students working for higher degrees or diplomas; b) women, not necessarily so engaged, who wish to re-equip themselves for professional careers by advanced study, or by obtaining higher qualifications".

The Dining Group as before continued to scan the Regent House list for names of women eligible to become members and to invite them to join. Again, and for many years to come, we asked the men's colleges for the names of their women supervisors and, if not already members of a college, offered them hospitality. We participated in a meeting organised by the Provost of King's College on the variety of problems that faced supervisors. We also, after years of indecision, agreed upon a name for ourselves.

Naming a college seems to be a difficult operation unless there has been a very large donation which makes it pleasant and appropriate to name it after the donor. In other cases there is a temptation to delay as long as possible in the hope that a fine benefactor may appear. I think that this could have been the case with both the Dining Group and with New Hall. I well remember the many discussions we had at the start of New Hall while

38 The College of which Margaret Braithwaite's husband is a Fellow.

I was on its Council. Should we choose a geographical name like Girton and Newnham Colleges which were both called after the villages in which they were built? But the third women's college did not at first know where it was going to be. In the end the forthright but unromantic name of New Hall was accepted. The Dining Group suffered from similar difficulties, and had made several earlier attempts. At the time when we were hoping to have the use of the Hall of Pythagoras, we thought we might name the Group after that building. Later we considered names of laudable and adventurous women and Mary Kingsley was one of those suggested.

Finally, by general agreement, the choice of the new name was "inspired by a wish to adopt as patron a remarkable woman of very recent times: Lucy Cavendish (1841–1925)"[39]. She was born a Lyttelton and shared that family's strong concern for education. She married Lord Frederick Cavendish, which gave her a connection with Cambridge, since both his father and brother were Chancellors of the University. After the tragedy of her husband's assassination in Phoenix Park, Dublin in 1882, she worked hard and raised money for a variety of causes for which she cared. These included helping in the founding of the Girls Public Day School Trust and the Old Vic Theatre. She was appointed, in 1894, to the Royal Commission on Secondary Education and in April 1904 was awarded the first Honorary Degree ever to be conferred by Leeds University. Her courage, warm sympathy and disarming wit are said to have endeared her to all types of people. Margaret Braithwaite was fortunate to have her as a great aunt, but this fact did not determine the decision.

As soon as the Dining Group had made its choice, the President wrote to the Duke of Devonshire asking for permission to use the name of Lucy Cavendish. This he readily gave and sent a small personal donation with his good wishes. The Society of Women Members of the Regent House who are not Fellows of Colleges, usually known as the Dining Goup, became the 'Lucy Cavendish Collegiate Society'.

Another report concerning societies for graduates was published by the University Council of the Senate in March 1964. This was entitled 'Amendments of the statutory provisions for colleges and other collegiate institutions' and recommended that Statute H, the relevant Statute, should become much more flexible. The amendments were to have widespread implications. They allowed the University, for the first time, to recognise colleges composed wholly of graduates among its 'Approved Foundations', whereas formerly it could recognise only those educating undergraduates. Further, these Foundations would no longer need to have their members all of one sex and would not necessarily have students at all. Secondly, and of more importance to Lucy Cavendish, was the creation of a new category, to

39 From a letter from K.Wood-Legh and Eileen Clifford to the editor of Cambridge Review of 2.5.1964. Her name was also mentioned in 1884 as a possible Mistress of Girton College (Mary Gladstone papers).

be known as 'Approved Societies'. This would give the University "power to recognise institutions of a less formal and more experimental character than is implied by an Approved Foundation" (Reporter 1963/4, p.1174). This new category we welcomed with joy for it seemed that it offered a niche for us and so removed one of the obstacles to our development.

As a result of the greater flexibility, the three colleges, Caius, St. John's and Trinity, who were already planning to found the first graduate college, were at once able to apply for University recognition for their proposed offspring, Darwin College. This recognition was granted in July 1964 and, as sufficient funds were being provided by the parent colleges and the Max Rayne Foundation, development was soon under way[40]. The University itself was also preparing plans to found a graduate college which was to have special care, by means of Reserved Fellowships, for University officers who had no other college attachment. The plan received approval in May 1965 and as the University undertook to give it a substantial grant for ten years, it too was able to start its development[41]. Some time later it received a very handsome benefaction from the Wolfson Foundation and changed its name from University to Wolfson College.

Shortly after Darwin College was recognised by the University, Clare College announced its intention to "promote within the college a Society for Graduates to be known as Clare Hall, which will be open to men and women and of which the Fellows will be Bye-Fellows of Clare College". Again money from the founding college and from two foundations[42], was assured and building soon started. The new college, officially recognised in February 1966, aimed to give particular care to academic visitors to the University, by inviting them into Visiting Fellowships. Next to seek University recognition was St. Edmund's House. This institution had been founded in 1896 under a Roman Catholic Trust and was regarded by the University as a 'House of Residence'. In October 1963 St. Edmund's had declared its wish to help the University with the non-Fellow problem and, as a result of the new amendments to Statute H, it could become an Approved Society. Its large and valuable buildings were evidence that it had suitable financial standing to be so recognised.

40 A document issued on the occasion of the opening of the Rayne Building and Dining Hall in 1969 states that the Founding Colleges undertook to provide jointly an initial capital sum of £25,000, and a sum of £15,000 annually for the first ten years. In 1964 the Max Rayne Foundation gave a benefaction of £500,000.
41 The University agreed,(Reporter 19644/5,p.1618), to give a grant of £15,000 for 2 years followed by £20,000 for 8 years.
42 Clare College provided the land and a sum of £450,000 and gifts of £175,000 and £200,000 were made by the Ford Foundation and the Old Dominion Foundation for the establishment of Visiting and Research Fellowships. (from an undated publication)

7. Progress of Lucy Cavendish Collegiate Society

With all this successful activity and with graduate societies sprouting-up all around us, we may perhaps be forgiven for having had a certain feeling of being by-passed and left far behind. Here we were, we who had played no small part in introducing the new idea of collegiate societies, still just as we had always been, a vigorous society filled with ideas, but with no possessions other than a capital of about £3,000 and a Visitors' Book. However, we continued actively to take part in University discussions in the Senate House and in writing in the Cambridge Review to show that we were still working hard to achieve our aims.

The main task was to complete the Trust Deed and an outline of 'Principal Suggested Regulations' by which Lucy Cavendish should be governed so that we could prepare our third application for University recognition. Discussions on these topics continued and there were consultations with our Trustees and with the Registrary. Finally, in November 1964, the draft documents, with a covering memorandum from the Trustees was sent to the Council of the Senate. The reply from the Registrary said that "no formal decisions were taken on the application pending further consideration of the question of accommodation for the Society and of the principle of using University funds to assist collegiate societies which were not established by the University; but the Council remained sympathetic to the Society". The application had not been turned down, only put into abeyance and further discussion with the Registrary was invited. This was good news, but more encouraging was the unofficial information, given during discussions, that though no money, even for the salary of a Head, would be forthcoming, it seemed that help in other forms might be given by the University. Further we heard that the Department of Estate Management was being asked to find premises for us, irrespective of whether recognition was granted by the University. Such recognition however would automatically make us a charity.

Other points which needed clearing before the application could go further concerned the title for the Head and the proposed Associate Membership. The decisions we took were that the Head should be called 'the President' and the category of Associates should be regarded as an internal domestic matter which did not appear in the Outline of Suggested Regulations.

Ever hopeful, we then began to consider what arrangements should be made for the first admission of students since we had specifically said that we wished to have graduate students. The sub-committee set up to consider the matter recommended that the first intake should not be more than 15 in number, with a rough balance between those reading Arts and those reading Science. This intake might have up to one-third of graduates from overseas and should include older women who had not pursued careers after graduation. The provision of a Combination Room and help in finding living

32

accommodation, were considered essential so confirming our urgent need for premises.

At this point I went on sabbatical leave with my husband to Australia to continue our field work on Sea-cows, this time the Dugong of the Pacific and Indian Oceans rather than the Manatee of the Atlantic. I was away from April to late August 1965 and my tasks as Secretary were kindly and ably taken on by Joan Liversidge, helped by Marion Clegg.

During this time came the wonderful news that premises for Lucy Cavendish had been found. The end of the long search had been brought about by a friend of the college mentioning to our President that Magdalene College was starting to rehabilitate its dilapidated cottages in Northampton Street. She at once wrote to the Master of the College, then Sir Henry Willink, saying that she noted with interest the work being done and then asked if there would be any room available for Lucy Cavendish. She got a welcoming reply and the long and the short of it was that the University then took a ten-year lease from Magdalene of three of the cottages (numbers 16–18) and most generously gave it to us rent free. With the money that they received from the lease Magdalene was able to recondition the property so that when we moved out after ten years they would be left with good lettable buildings. As the cottages could not be ready until Easter 1966, the University offered us the use of two rooms on the groundfloor of 20 Silver Street, which we gratefully accepted.

More good news followed quickly. We heard that the Registry had been instructed to draw up a report on the Lucy Cavendish Collegiate Society with a view to its recognition by the University. The report, which appeared on 9 June, 1965 (Reporter 1964/65, p1942), included a brief account of our history, our functions, and the reasons why the Council now recommended that we should be granted recognition. Mention was made of the fact that we had "more than once brought to the attention of the University fruitful ideas about ways in which the collegiate structure of the University might be extended and adapted to present-day needs. A notable example is the Memorandum submitted . . . in connexion with the Report of the Bridges Syndicate (Reporter 1961/62, p1733)." We had shown ourselves "ready to accept wider responsibilities", for example by offering facilities to women who were "supervising students in the colleges or were engaged in other academical work in Cambridge". We now wished to enlarge our activities and believed that we could make a contribution to the solution of the problem, now recognised as of national importance, arising "from the fact that insufficient use is made of the services of professional women whose careers have been interrupted by family or other commitments". This contribution could be by "offering some women the opportunity of re-equipping themselves by advanced study or by obtaining higher qualifications".

Note was taken by the Council that we had, till then, developed "on the basis of very slender financial resources, mostly derived from regular

33

contributions and donations" from our members. We had not so far felt able to seek more widely for financial assistance since, without University recognition, we were not a "legal charity". Other handicaps had been the lack of premises of our own and the "informality" of our constitution. Now that premises had been found, Trustees appointed and Trust Deed prepared, the Council considered that, though we differed "in many ways from the Collegiate Institutions to which the University is accustomed", we would be "suitably constituted for recognition as an Approved Society". Members of the University were reminded that this was the new category of institutions established in 1964 which gave the University the power to recognise "institutions of a less formal and more experimental character than is implied by an Approved Foundation".

The report ended with the recommendation that "from the date on which a Trust Deed in terms approved by the Council of the Senate is executed, the Lucy Cavendish Collegiate Society be recognised as an Approved Society and be governed by the following regulations: . . . " These regulations specify that Fellows and students of the Society should have the same status as those of other colleges, except that, in line with other graduate foundations, it should not admit undergraduates.

The report then went forward to the Discussion held on 13 July 1965 where criticism or comments could have delayed or hindered our progress. Fortunately not a word was said and the recommendations were duly and formally approved by the University by a Grace dated 31 July 1965. At last Lucy Cavendish Collegiate Society, as a corporate body, was part of Cambridge University. In her notes Anna Bidder, as President, records with gratitude the large amount of help the Registrary had given us in our request for recognition and continues, "I should like here to pay tribute to the Council of the Senate for having recommended it (i.e. recognition) and to the University for having accepted it because I think it was a generous and adventurous thing to do."

The final step was to get the Trust Deed signed by all those who had become Trustees. (Appendix V). Seven had signed by mid-August, but the Provost of King's was abroad. With his signature on 15 September 1965 Lucy Cavendish Collegiate Society became at once an Approved Society of the University, a legal entity and a charity. All this and the promise of premises too! It was a momentous time indeed and I arrived back from Australia in time to share in the rejoicing.

II. After Recognition

1. 1965 to 1966. The Intermediate Year.

My first suggestion, on hearing that we had rooms for an office, was that we should at once get an answering machine. This was promptly countered by Margaret Braithwaite who insisted that we should certainly have a full-time secretary from the beginning. How right she was, for as soon as term started we were extremely busy.

As early as 29th July 1965, in anticipation of the Trust Deed becoming effective, the Trustees at their first meeting resolved that the existing members of the Society should form the Governing Body of the new College. As members of a Governing Body we became Fellows and had the same status and privileges in the University as the Fellows of all other Colleges (see Appendix VI). The Trustees also determined that there should be a Council and that, for the first year, this should consist of the first body of Fellows with the exception of any who signified that they did not wish to serve. Anna Bidder was appointed President for one year, it being understood that, owing to her scientific commitments, she was willing "to hold this office for only this specified length of time". The other officers were, until December 1965, to be those of the former informal Society, with the addition of Jay Evans as Junior Bursar.

Thus we had a formal legal framework as well as accommodation when we moved into our rooms in Silver Street on 12th October 1965. We had also found by then an admirable secretary in Sharon Lowes who entered into our spirit of excitement and enjoyed setting up an office and temporary base. Our premises consisted of two newly-decorated ground floor rooms, each furnished with a desk, a desk chair, an upright chair, a filing cabinet, a telephone and a metal wastepaper basket. We hired a typewriter and set about ordering stationery and other necessities. On the advice of my eldest son, then an architectural student, we chose A4 size paper and were the first College in Cambridge to do so, while the rest continued for some while with the older foolscap and quarto. One of our rooms was kept for the Secretary and the other mainly for my use as Tutor and Secretary of the G.B., with filing accommodation for the President.[43]

Although the Trustees remained responsible for all decisions, it had long been agreed that they would "accept recommendations from the Society". The first meeting of the Governing Body, also held before our recognition by the University had been approved, took place in Anna's flat about three

43 Also the President was invited to use the services of the College Secretary for her professional or private matters to allow her more time for her zoological work as well as looking after the affairs of the College.

weeks after the first meeting of Trustees. The President reported that preparations for an appeal for funds to the Cambridge Colleges were already started. A document to be sent to all women members of the Regent House was also needed to tell them of the College's activities and inviting new members to join. Internal business included discussion on the titles for College officers. The title of Bursar was given to Nora Willson (formerly Treasurer), and that of Senior Tutor was to be offered to me on my return from Australia late in August 1965. I gladly accepted the Tutorship, but was allowed to drop the 'Senior' as there was no other.

This then was the general situation when the University term began in October 1965. For the first time our notices appeared in the University Reporter, our names were included in the List of Resident Members and we were accepted as members of the Colleges', Bursars', and Stewards' Committees and the University's Tutorial Representatives. We also joined the Cambridge Intercollegiate Graduate Scheme.

The informal Society finally wound itself up on 12th October by deciding that it should cease to exist after 31st December, 1965. This meeting took place in Harvey Court after the weekly dinner and immediately following it the same people met as the Governing Body. Enquiries had shown that 17 out of the 22 Founding Fellows wished to serve on the Council and this new body was asked to consider and recommend procedures for the appointment or election of the Head, Fellows, Officers and Council members and their tenure.

Three days later the Trustees met in the Department of Agriculture by the invitation of Prof. Hutchinson. The main business was financial, including banking arrangements and comments on the proposed appeal document. Margaret Bottrall was appointed Secretary to the Trustees.

Five days later the Council met for the first time and thereafter it met every fortnight during each term. The chief concern of this first meeting was to set up committees to run the various aspects of the new College. The particular committees established were Tutorial; House, which was to prepare for our move to Northampton Street; Standing, to start work on a constitution; and Editorial, to be concerned with publicity. During the first three terms the Council and the Trustees usually met alternately. The two groups worked very closely together and suggestions from each were discussed by the other before finally being approved by the Trustees. Gradually an increasing number and type of responsibilities was handed over by the Trustees to the College.

There was much work to be done and much to learn. Several people have said to me in recent years that they never believed that a group of women without special experience of administration, and without money, could succeed in founding a new College. But actually we were not as inexperienced as they supposed. All of us were working in the University, many of us had taken part in teaching and entrance examinations in other Colleges, and all of us had friends or husbands in other parts of Cambridge who could tell us how things were done there. In addition, everyone we came across in our dealings with the University was unstintedly helpful and encouraging. We, as an Approved Society, had been recognised by the University as an "institution of a less formal and more experimental character than is implied by an Approved Foundation". We were determined that we should indeed continue to think out our aims, constitution and development most carefully and not just follow the pattern of existing Colleges. This meant that at times we did not seem quite to fit the picture. Never did we get the flat reply "No, you cannot do that," but always the attitude "Well, let us see if that would be possible." This attitude was an integral part of our success.

Apart from arranging matters within the College, the main activity that first term concerned our appeal for funds to the Colleges in Cambridge. Many drafts were prepared, together with estimates of costs, and the final document was sent to the Heads of all the Colleges in December 1965 with a covering letter signed by the Chairman of Trustees and the President. This Appeal Memorandum gave a brief account of the history of the College, its plans, its structure and its immediate financial needs. These needs were an "initial capital outlay of £3,000 and estimated minimal annual costs for seven years totalling £30,000 . . . ". A later and wider appeal would be made for "the cost of expected developments".

At the end of the term the Council reported on its activities at an informal meeting of the Governing Body and the Trustees confirmed that "the College had collegiate status for the purpose of tax exemption". The first mention of the Calouste Gulbenkian Foundation, which was to mean so much in the future, was made by one of the Trustees, Professor Annan, who offered to write to them to see if they could be interested in the work of the new Lucy Cavendish College.

During the second term, the Lent Term of 1966, there was a proliferation of memoranda. These covered a wide range of subjects, including details of Fellowship and how Fellows should be elected and re-elected, procedures for the admission of students and arrangement of fees, organisation of the Council and its committees and written comments on many of the original memoranda. As a result, much thought and discussion were generated and decisions made. These made it possible for the Trustees to approve an agreed procedure for the election of new Fellows, for our committee structure to be re-organised, and for our first student, Elizabeth Dupré, to be admitted to read for a PhD[44]. Meanwhile the Trustees appointed K. Wood-Legh, sine die, to the special office of Pro-President and invited her to attend all Trustee meetings in a non-voting capacity. They also confirmed in office for three years the Vice-President (Braithwaite), the Bursar (Willson), Junior Bursar (Evans),

---

44 Her chief interest was in the changing sensibility and thought between 1660 and 1714 and she planned to edit Burnet's "History of my own Times" for Blackwells.

Steward (Clifford) and Tutor (Bertram). £500 a year was allotted to me, as Secretary to the Council, as well as Tutor, and so responsible for much of the day-to-day administration.

These were all internal matters, but external development was also taking place. Donations from the Colleges were beginning to arrive as a result of our appeal. At a "distinctly encouraging" meeting with Mr. J. Thornton, then Secretary to the Calouste Gulbenkian Foundation, in our Silver Street office (with the President sitting on the upturned metal waste paper basket) we were invited to draft a special appeal to his Trustees. Then came a letter, addressed to the Senior Tutor of all the Colleges, which caused great interest. It was from the Registrary (dated 17.2.66) and contained information about ways in which the University Grants Committee, after its quinquennial visit, "would welcome development at Cambridge". These included "the further extension of graduate activities" so that any increase in student numbers would be "proportionately greater among graduate students than among undergraduates". Hope was also expressed that "any increase of the undergraduate population in Cambridge would have the effect of increasing the percentage of women undergraduates". These statements raised in our minds the possibility that we might be invited to become a fourth women's undergraduate College, and we at once wrote that we would "welcome an opportunity to contribute to the increase in women undergraduates in Cambridge". We added that we believed that we could "offer the advantages of an established women's community of wide interests and experience into which undergraduates could be brought with profit to themselves and to the University". Further we hoped that the Council of the Senate would endorse our view that we should develop our work for graduate students as rapidly as possible. The reply from the Registrary (dated 4.5.66) said that the Council of the Senate appreciated our desire to be helpful and shared our view about rapid development of our work for graduate students. It did not, however, think that it was an appropriate time for us to consider taking undergraduates which would involve changes in the basic terms on which we had so recently been granted recognition by the University. This reply brought no surprise, though some disappointment, but it had given us the opportunity to show the University that we were both confident and willing to be helpful.

At the beginning of the May Term 1966 the election of new Fellows was an important part of the College's business. By general agreement it was decided that up to five new Fellows should be chosen, from outside or within the University, and that they should be elected by a single Aye or No paper vote, the electors on this occasion to be the members of the Council. Tenure should be for three years in the first instance. Later the procedure for re-election should be that the Founding Fellows should be re-elected by the Trustees and any other Fellow by the body which first elected her. Over the question of retirement, there was a difference of opinion within the Trustees. The Vice-President, strongly supported by the President, proposed that Fellows

38

should retire at 70[45], while some others thought it should be at the University retiring age, then 67. The reason put forward for the later age was that most of those concerned "would be women who had perforce lost some years of academic life in mid-career". In fact it became the practice in Lucy Cavendish for Fellows to retire from active membership of the Governing Body at 70. There is much variation among the Cambridge Colleges, some having certain classes of Fellows on their Governing Bodies for life.

On 20.4.66 four Fellows were elected by the Council: Ethel Cruickshank, who had been a strong supporter of the Dining Group in its earliest days; Jane Jack, whose subject was English; Olga Kennard, a crystallographer (now a Fellow of the Royal Society), and Marie Lawrence, a Physical Anthropologist. A fortnight later Mary Hay, a Physiologist, was also elected. These elections were reported to the Trustees and to the Governing Body which accepted also other reports from the Council.

By this time it had become apparent that there were too many layers in our administration leading to duplication and unnecessary meetings. I wrote a memorandum, dated 15.4.66, suggesting that the Council should cease to function leaving the College to be run by the Governing Body alone, subject to the over-riding responsibility of the Trustees. The arguments in favour of the single body were that it would make administration simpler and less time-consuming, that it was not sensible to have a second body almost identical in composition to the Governing Body, particularly when there had not been any formal delegation of function from that body, and that it would give all the Fellows equal opportunities to take part in the building of the College and its constitution. This reasoning was accepted and the Council met for the last time on 1st June 1966 and silently disappeared. In May 1966 the Trustees re-appointed Anna Bidder as President for a further year, again at her wish not to commit herself for two years as had been hoped, and they invited Joan Liversidge to be Praelector, the officer responsible for formal occasions in the College and in the University.

During this academic year of 1965–66 we continued to dine once a week in Harvey Court and our Governing Body meetings were still held there. The average number dining each week was 12 for the Michaelmas Term and 17 for the Lent Term. We continued also to offer hospitality in the form of Dining Privileges to women supervisors working in the men's Colleges and to some others. As we had done in the past, we invited all women members of the Regent House who were not Fellows of Colleges to dine with us if they were interested. These, of course, were already members of the University, as were those among the supervisors who were Cambridge graduates. However, some who were teaching in the Colleges were graduates of other Universities and, as they did not hold any official post in Cambridge University, they were not included amongst its members. By offering them membership of

45 In a memorandum by Margaret Braithwaite dated 7.5.1966.

the College, now formally recognised, they were able to become members of the University. This was helpful, but did not go far enough. Much thought was therefore given as to what special categories of membership, apart from Fellowship, were needed if the College was to be able to carry out its aim of helping women, in addition to those needing degrees or other qualifications, back into academic life and forwarding their careers.

As early as December 1965, in our Appeal Memorandum, we stated that we intended to create new senior categories which would "carry a status intermediate between Fellows and holders of dining rights". In April 1966 the President and Vice-President met with the supervisors on two occasions to consider how best the College could help them. Lively discussions, it seems, took place and it became clear that their needs varied greatly. As a result of these meetings some of the supervisors[46] undertook to make further investigations. Two of them wrote a long interim report including comments on the general problems of women returning to work. Two others volunteered to interview all their number to learn more of the position and this offer was gratefully accepted. Another, Mindele Treip, also prepared a memorandum defining a new category of 'Senior Membership'. She proposed that women with dining privileges should be able "to apply for Senior Membership in the College, if they feel such would benefit their work." Their applications should then be considered by a committee of existing Senior Members and Fellows and, if found suitable, the candidate could be elected a Senior Member. The types of facilities which would be most helpful to them were mentioned. Appreciation of these proposals was expressed and, after discussion, a resolution that "the College re-affirm its intention to establish at some date a category of Senior Members who are not Fellows" was carried unanimously.

In line with these suggestions, I wrote a brief memorandum proposing that, as the usual method of becoming a full member of a Cambridge College was a fee-paying period of work under the aegis of that College, any Senior Members of Lucy Cavendish should be asked to pay a fee. It also suggested that such non-Fellow members should have a voice in the affairs of the College[47]. These proposals were discussed on 15.6.66 and agreed in principle. The fee agreed was £8 per term and included three free dinners. The maximum number of Senior Members in the first place was to be 30 and their applications for this membership must be supported by two Fellows. In the event 12 were elected in September 1966 and their names were included in the Residents' List the next academic year.

Considerable discussion took place about the name of this category, including

46 These were: Esther Goody, a social anthropologist who was elected a Fellow and College Lecturer in New Hall in April 1966; Leonore Lockwood and Elaine Sofer, both social scientists, wrote "A Preliminary Report for the Lucy Cavendish Collegiate Society" on 25.4.1966; Mindele Treip's memo was dated 23.4.66. She later became a Fellow and College Lecturer of Lucy Cavendish.
47 College circular No.44/666 of 13.6.66.

suggestions such as Bye-Fellow, Fellow-Commoner etc., but in the end they remained 'Senior Members'. They became a most valuable group, recognised as an integral part of the College in the draft statutes prepared in 1976 and agreed by the Trustees and Governing Body. Our Senior Members later provided Fellows, not only for their own College, but also for the women's Colleges and men's as they became co-residential. By 1979 24 members of the Dining Group and the Lucy Cavendish Collegiate Society had been elected to Fellowships in other Cambridge and Oxford Colleges.

By the summer of 1966 the young College had made arrangements for its membership and its procedures, but, as noted by the Trustees, its growth in these spheres "appeared to have outstripped the growth of its finances". The result of the appeal to the Colleges had been disappointing. It produced only £4,315, a sum rather smaller than that raised from the members of Lucy Cavendish and their friends, who had been so generous in taking out covenants.[48]

Much thought was given to further fund-raising. An application to the Council of the Senate asked if the University "would guarantee for five years our basic running expenses (£3,082 per annum) so that the limited funds at our disposal can be devoted to furthering the work among the women resident in Cambridge". Regrettably the Council[49] felt unable to recommend this guarantee, but they did make certain helpful statutory arrangements. These allowed Colleges which voluntarily contributed money to Lucy Cavendish College to regard their gifts as deductible items when calculating their liability for University contribution. Hope was expressed that this might induce more Colleges to respond to our appeal and others to enlarge their donations.

In other directions approaches were being made or planned to seven Foundations or Trusts. Discussion was continuing actively with the Calouste Gulbenkian Foundation and Anna Bidder was personally approaching the friends and colleagues of her late father to form a George Bidder Memorial Fund. As he was our first benefactor, the Fellows wanted to have a room in the College named after him and contributors to the Memorial Fund were invited, if they wished, to earmark their gifts towards the furnishing of our Combination Room, to be called the George Bidder Room. Many did so and despite subsequent house moves the results of their generosity are still evident in our present George Bidder Room. These include the "charming extendable table round which, at full extension, the Governing Body can just dispose themselves"[50]. The Governing Body is now too large, but the Trustees and many committees still sit round it under the portrait of George Bidder on the wall above them.

As the College developed, organised from our temporary two rooms in

---

48 These sums were in addition to the £3,144 which we already owned at the time of recognition.
49 Letter from the Registrary dated 25.7.66.
50 Anna Bidder's notes.(see no.7)

41

Silver Street, restoration of the promised houses in Northampton Street[51] was going ahead. The Junior Bursar, Jay Evans (together with Mr. Robinson and Mr. Davis of the Department of Estate Management) was in charge of this work and her Day Book of the period between 7.8.65 and 7.8.68 gives detailed accounts of the progress. The 18th century houses were stripped down to mere skeletons and re-built so that they could first be suitable for us and then later become residential accommodation for research students from Magdalene College.

The completion of the building work took longer than expected, the delays being chiefly caused by difficulties over the electrical installations. The heating system was by off-peak electric heaters and warm air ducts and intermittently gave trouble both then and in the future. It is also clear from the Day Book that there were the usual kinds of awkwardness: e.g. "The two storage heaters delivered last Thursday are unsuitable and therefore cannot be installed"; "Too many walls have been painted zephyr, instead of silver grey . . . "; "Had 18 keys cut: none of these fit"!

The steward, Eileen Clifford, also played a major part in helping to acquire, by buying and borrowing, the requisite furniture and fittings. Many gifts and loans were made, including a handsome donation from Etheljohn Lindgren of eight crates of splendid yellow china, Suzanne Faience of Royal Copenhagen Porcelain. The ground floor of the houses contained the George Bidder Room, parlour and kitchen, while the upper three rooms in one provided small offices for the President, Tutor and Secretary, and the other had three residential rooms.

At last, on 8th June 1966, we took possession and moved in the following day. A week later we held there our first formal occasion at which the President, helped by the Praelector, formally admitted the first 22 Fellows to their Fellowships. The ceremony had been carefully planned and, in full academic dress, in the order in which we had joined the Society, we swore the oath of loyalty.[52] We then signed the Fellows' Book and moved to a wine and cheese party before our first Governing Body meeting in our new home.

Some weeks after the move our admirable first secretary, Sharon Lowes, decided that she wanted to travel abroad and so resigned. We were very sorry to lose her and her infectious enthusiasm.

The rest of the Summer of 1966 passed uneventfully until just at the end

---

51 There were originally three houses, Nos.16-18, but No.16 disappeared in the re-building: the remaining two were inter-communicating on the ground floor. The Day Book of the Junior Bursar is in the College archives.

52 The Oath of Loyalty reads: I, _____ elected Fellow of Lucy Cavendish Collegiate Society do hereby promise that I will loyally observe the statutes and good customs of the College, and in all things endeavour to the utmost of my power to promote the peace, honour and well-being of the College as a place of education, religion, learning and research.

of September the Barrow and Geraldine S. Cadbury Trust gave us a generous donation of £500 a year for three years. This delighted us, strengthened our confidence and made a happy start for the next academic year.

2.   1966–1970 –
Lucy Cavendish as a Graduate College

For the next four years Anna Bidder remained our President and skilfully led us through much activity and thought. Perhaps the most important happenings during this period were the growing number of students and the rapid expansion of the Senior Membership within the College, the search for funds, and the plans for more provision for women undergraduates in the University.

As soon as the Michaelmas Term of 1966 started we welcomed the arrival of our first residential research student. She was Margaret Seay and she came from the United States. We were all delighted that someone from so far away should, among the Cambridge Colleges, have chosen the new and small Lucy Cavendish. We asked her what had particularly appealed to her and what had made her make us her choice. To our surprise she laughed and said that as she did not know much about any of the Colleges she had just shut her eyes and chosen us with a pin! So much for our belief that our fame had already spread across the Atlantic. She quickly settled in with enthusiasm to read for a PhD in mathematics ('Numbers Theory') and to enjoy Cambridge. She was a great asset to the College, liked by everyone and full of ideas.[53] The present College scarf was her design.

Others soon followed, but the numbers did not increase as rapidly as expected and never reached the figure of 100 which in 1970 we told the University was the maximum we could look after. The need for more provision for research students in Cambridge, particularly for women, which had earlier been so pressing had to some extent evaporated. The reasons for this were twofold: first the economic climate was changing somewhat and grants for research were harder to come by, and secondly the other new graduate Colleges were starting to take women as well as men as research students.

The graduate students varied greatly in their needs and interests. Some wanted to read for a PhD, but others worked for other higher degrees, diplomas or certificates. Altogether, between 1968 and 1980, the total number who had gained higher qualifications was 84, but there had never been more than 33 at any one time. Most had chosen to come to Lucy Cavendish because of its special concern for those who had a break in their careers or wanted

53 She intermitted 1967/68, then married (Oglesby) and withdrew in April 1968.

to change direction. They therefore tended to be somewhat older than the normal research student and certainly brought added vigour to the College. As their Tutor, I was mainly responsible for any matters which concerned their relations with the University, but there were few real problems because they fitted in to the well-established procedures for graduate students in general. Within the College they were welcomed by everyone and they established themselves so easily that mention of them scarcely appears in the Governing Body minutes. By May 1970 they had started an internal Students' Association.

By contrast the development and affairs of the Senior Membership appeared on the agenda of practically every meeting of the Governing Body during 1967 and frequently afterwards. Many memoranda were prepared and discussed on matters such as their numbers, methods of selection, tenure and other constitutional arrangements. Most important was the subject of their relationship with the Governing Body for they were a special group not found in other Colleges. They became increasingly involved in the life of the College and in the discussions on its future policies. In May 1967 the position was formalised by the creation of a Joint Committee, consisting of nine Fellows and nine Senior Members, which was to have advisory but not executive powers. (Later, graduate students were also represented on this committee.) Additionally, the Senior Members reported regularly to the Governing Body and a summary report of each Governing Body meeting was sent to them. By 1970 they numbered 26, the highest number at any one time, while the Fellowship then contained 30. Between 1966 and 1980 a total of 76 women were admitted to Senior Membership.[54] Their length of time as Senior Members varied greatly: some stayed for long periods; others went to Fellowships or other occupations in the College or elsewhere and some became graduate students taking higher qualifications.

Finance continued as a major preoccupation of this period and our approaches to various Foundations and Trusts[55] were mostly unsuccessful. However, there was one pleasing gift from the Hilden Trust which gave £250 per annum for three years to help a graduate student. This award was given to our first non-residential student, Elizabeth Dupre.

In January 1967 a survey of the finances of the College, prepared by me, concluded "it would seem that, running at the present level and without any additional non-recurrent expenditure, the College can continue for at least two years (the period of the Cadbury grant of £500 p.a.) without encroaching on its capital." The minutes record that although they "noted with relief that the College is just solvent", the Trustees, in consultation with the Vice-Chancellor, thought it advisable to make another appeal within the University. This time the appeal was to be addressed to the Members of the Senate and

54 As many as 33 of them were scientists. Other categories of membership were also being established.
55 These included Rowntree, Nuffield, Carnegie, Lankelly, Leverhulme, Ford and Hopkins.

the Regent House (i.e. all resident MAs), and sent in the coming Easter Term. At the same time a letter was to be sent to the Council of the Senate "not asking for a specific sum of money, but submitting a budget".

The possibility of asking professional advice for this appeal was discussed but rejected, and a special fund-raising committee was set up by the Governing Body. Much hard work was done by this committee, particularly by K. Wood-Legh and Marie Lawrence (later to become a Tutor). The Governing Body and Trustees also gave a great deal of time and thought to the preparation of a suitable appeal document. During the discussions the Trustees stressed that the object of the appeal was "to enable Lucy Cavendish to expand its experimental work among Senior Members" and that they considered it to be their "continuing duty and desire to promote the academic interests of women graduates, especially those whose careers have been interrupted". The work was complicated, however, by an uncertainty as to what part Lucy Cavendish might play in developments which might occur in the University. On 14th April 1967 the President reported to the Governing Body that "An unforeseen development indicates the possibility of a considerable addition to the planning of the Lucy Cavendish Collegiate Society . . . "[56]. Four weeks later she reported that it had become clear that any possibility of a development in the plans of the College would not be crystallised in the immediate future and that the Trustees, therefore, recommended that the College should issue the appeal at once. It was not until mid-June that the President was able, and then only in the strictest confidence, to let the Governing Body know what lay behind these uncertainties (see p.).

Under these circumstances, with the Fellows being "keyed up to action and then damped down without information"[57], it is perhaps not surprising that it was the sixth draft of the appeal document that was finally approved by the Governing Body on 10th May 1967. The Vice-Chancellor, the Chairman of Trustees and the President then signed the document and it was circulated to about 3,000 Cambridge MAs. By the end of the year a sum, including covenants, of about £4,300 had been received as a result. This came from 177 donors, many of whom subsequently renewed their covenants, and was about the same sum as that received from the earlier appeal to the Colleges. It was allocated for grants of various kinds for Senior Members who were then invited to apply for money, particularly to help towards expenses incurred through original work. These awards were made by a special committee, were much appreciated and helped "to build up the corporate life of the College".[58]

Soon after the appeal was launched, Anna Bidder was again in touch with the Calouste Gulbenkian Foundation. The Secretary of the Foundation, Mr. J.C. Thornton, had suggested that £2,000–£3,000 might be available for three years "to further scholarly enterprises". For the next six months there was

56 Quoted from Circulars Nos.56/467 and 71/567. (to line 23)
57 From a letter from Anna Bidder to the Vice-Chancellor, dated 5.5.67.
58 The first awards are recorded in Reporter 1967/8,p.1054.

much discussion[59] within the College on the exact form, function and duration of such a grant. Mr. Thornton explained that the Foundation never gave grants to individuals, only for the furtherance of schemes, and that they were seldom, if ever, repeated. Later the offer was increased to £5,000 for three years which could be spread over five years if this arrangement made it more suitable for Fellowships. In their final document of application for such a grant the Trustees and Governing Body specified that the object would be "to help to enable Lucy Cavendish to establish a Fund to assist women graduates (particularly married women and others whose careers have been interrupted) who, on returning to active University life, wish to improve the quality of their teaching and research". In this way they might also improve or add to the teaching force in Cambridge. The application was sent late in October 1967 and by the end of the year we heard that it had been successful: the agreed sum of £15,000 had been granted "to establish a College Fund for assisting research".

The receipt of this benefaction was of inestimable value to the College in its early formative years. It enabled us not only to start at once to help individuals to re-establish themselves, but also to attract to the College able women from all over Britain. A special committee was set up to plan in detail how the Fund should be administered and how the advertisements for the awards should be framed. Mr. Thornton himself took a great interest in the scheme and gave us much valuable help until his untimely death in June 1969.

The first advertisement appeared in 1968 in the Reporter (1967/8 p.1294) and in several national newspapers stating that up to three research Fellowships were to be offered and that "candidates must be women graduates who, by research, publication or otherwise, have shown their ability to do original work; their proposed field must be approved by the University". Up to three research studentships were also offered for "women graduates wishing to undertake post-graduate study". Both types of award were normally to be for 2-3 years and were "primarily designed for women whose professional careers have been interrupted by marriage or other causes and who wish to resume academic or other professional work".

The advertisement produced many enquiries, and finally 34 completed applications were received, 22 for Fellowships and 12 for Studentships. The references of 18 of these candidates were taken up, nine were interviewed and in June 1968 the Governing Body elected the first five research Fellows, one research student and gave a grant to another. Among the Fellows one, Mindele Treip, was already a Senior Member, but the others had no earlier connection with the College.[60] Though this first election was made by the Governing Body, a later decision was that an Awards Committee should be

59 Including an emergency meeting of the Governing Body on 29.8.67
60 The four were Helen Alderson, Hilda Davidson, Stephanie Dee and Janet Stein.

authorised to appoint the Research Fellows, subject to confirmation by the Governing Body. In reporting to the Gulbenkian Foundation on this first election, Anna Bidder in a letter told Mr. Thornton that "the field is very good — just what we hoped for — some very able women, and some heart-breaking histories!". Although the awards were small in terms of money, they gave much confidence and considerable status. One example she desribed was: "Mrs. Alderson, a Russian-born mathematician, came to see me starry-eyed. 'I had no idea you were giving me so much: all doors are open.' Her Professor, as soon as he heard (about her award), gave her a room in the maths lab." Others found that their families were much more willing to leave them undisturbed since if someone was actually paying them to do this writing, then it really must be important.

Despite earlier assertions, in September 1972, to our great satisfaction, the Gulbenkian Foundation did in fact renew our grant on the same terms as the original. This enabled the College to make research awards in the form of Fellowships, Studentships and Grants to as many as 50 women during the ten years of the benefaction. The interests of those holding awards lay in a wide range of subjects, including 12 in science. Five of the Research Fellows were subsequently elected to our Governing Body.[61] Most certainly the generosity of this Foundation played an important part in the development of the College.

In the Summer of 1967 the Chairman of Trustees had written to Anna Bidder saying that they unanimously wished to re-appoint her as President for a further three years from 1st October, but that they "understood that circumstances might arise in connection with your own affairs or with those of the College which might make you wish to resign earlier. We all very much hope that on this understanding you would feel able to accept." In her reply Anna expressed her warm appreciation of the invitation which she accepted subject to "the condition that she might make way for a suitable successor should one be found". She explained that as her official University work as a zoologist would terminate in 1970, she sincerely hoped that a successor would be found "in time for her to pursue her scientific studies at least during the last year of the period named."[62] The Governing Body were delighted by the re-appointment and unanimously expressed its gratitude, but she did serve the full three years and did not get her last year free for study.

The other College officers continued unchanged during the period except that the Bursarship changed hands in February 1967 when Nora Willson

---

61 These were Harriet Crawford, Hilda Davidson, Barbara Hayley, Janet Stein & Mindele Treip.
62 In a personal note to me Anna Bidder says what actually happened was that at a Trustee meeting Chase said (more or less) 'we can't go on like this – we must know where we are – I move that Dr.Bidder be appointed for another three years – Agreed? – Thank you, carried. I have no doubt that a proper exchange of letters followed, but I was completely bull-dosed into it – I was not even asked.

resigned and Joyce Linfoot was appointed in her place. She held that important post until 1979.[63]

Throughout the period in Northampton Street we continued to dine together once a week. At first we still met in Harvey Court, but even with the kindly subsidisation by Caius College (till December 1968) the meals were becoming rather expensive and other arrangements difficult, so we looked elsewhere. After considerable searching we found another happy arrangement whereby we dined in the pleasant Club Room in Churchill College and this lasted until 1974.

The first of a series of College dinners was held in Harvey Court in October 1966. This occasion developed over the years into an annual gathering of all Members of the College, both past and present. As numbers increased we moved first to the Old Kitchen at Trinity College, then to the Old Library of Emmanuel College and then to St. John's College.[64] Recently Annual Dinners have been in the Dining Hall of Churchill College.

Informal meals, including picnic lunches, played a useful part in our consolidation. House-warming parties, dessert and sherry parties all helped with publicity for the 1967 appeal. These, and other social occasions, took place in the George Bidder Room. This was our Combination Room and was managed by a committee consisting of Fellows, Senior Members and a representative of the students. The room was used by all members of the College, including also the two new categories we had introduced into our structure, namely Honorary Fellows and Honorary Members. Honorary Fellowship was designed for distinguished women not otherwise connected with the College. The first three invitations were sent in 1968 and during that Summer Dame Kathleen Lonsdale and Joyce Grenfell accepted, but the third, though sympathetic to our aims, felt unable to join us.[65] Honorary Membership included the Secretary of the Women's Appointment Board and some of the members of the old Dining Group who had become Fellows of other Colleges. Women supervisors from the men's Colleges continued to be offered hospitality.

By this time, 1968, the student numbers in the University as a whole had reached just over 10,000, of whom almost 2,000 were post-graduates. In 1938 the number had been just less than 6,000. This increase resulted from the rise in number of births after the war and in the number of girls and boys staying on at school and obtaining Advanced levels in the GCE examinations. Within the student population the poportion of women was still only just over 10% and there was a widespread wish to increase their number. It was in this connection that, during the first half of 1967, the highly confidential

63 An archivist, Dorothy Owen, was appointed in 1967 and Miss Barr became the College Solicitor.
64 The move to Emmanuel was in September 1965 and to St.Johns in 1977.
65 The third Honorary Fellow was Shirley Williams; the Secretary of the Women's Appointments Board was Joan Holgate and the early members were Carmen Blacker, Alice Heim & Edith Whetham

discussion between our President and the Vice-Chancellor took place (see p. 000). Apparently there had been the possibility of a large grant being offered by a Foundation[66] to start a new College in the building just vacated by the Theological College, Cheshunt, on its amalgamation with Westminster College.[67] Eventually in mid-June, Anna Bidder was able to tell the Governing Body, "I am now at liberty to say that the project on which reticence has for so long been forced upon me, was the possible utilisation of Cheshunt College as a fourth women undergraduates' College and the further possibility of Lucy Cavendish College being asked to be responsible for its formation. I am now informed that the scheme in that form has fallen through; the College is thus free both to continue its natural development as a graduate foundation and to consider the possibility of having undergraduates in the future. I am very grateful indeed for the forebearance which the whole College has shown during these difficult and frustrating weeks."

Certainly the whole subject was confidential and Anna remembers being congratulated by the Vice-Chancellor on the fact that there was no leak of any kind even though she had, with his leave, discussed the matter within one of our Governing Body meetings. However, in the event, nothing came of this particular idea and the building now belongs to the Freemasons.

Though there was some disappointment that the Cheshunt plan did not materialise there were still hopes that a fourth women's College would be founded. There was also much encouragement in the knowledge that the Vice-Chancellor considered us capable of looking after undergraduates. This being so the President believed that "the possibility of a fourth College for women undergraduates, organised by Lucy Cavendish College, still required urgent consideration". Both Trustees and Governing Body agreed, but at the same time passed resolutions that they "affirmed that funds which have been or shall be subscribed to the College as at present constituted cannot be diverted to other purposes". The general tone of these and other minutes show the determination that the first aims of the College, as stated at the time of our University recognition, should not be lost sight of if we took part in a larger scheme.

From this time on there were intermittent consultations and discussions between the President and the Vice-Chancellor about a fourth College and whether Lucy Cavendish could or should take undergraduates. On one occasion Anna Bidder asked whether there was any likelihood of University Grants Committee funds being available for a fourth women's College; on another the Vice-Chancellor made it clear that no guarantee could be given that any such scheme would involve our College. Finally, after a meeting on 29.1.68, the Governing Body was invited "to prepare a Memorandum . . . stating

66 Possibly Wolfson.
67 The Times' obituary, dated 8.11.64, of the Rev.Alan MacLeod, (former Principal of Westminster College) says he was a leader in bringing together Westminster and Cheshunt Colleges and linking them with the Cambridge Federation of Theological Colleges.

what contribution Lucy Cavendish College could make to the education of undergraduate women if they received an invitation from the University to do so." It was agreed that this memorandum should be undertaken as a matter of urgency in view of the fact that the formation of a fourth women's College was being actively discussed in the University. Professor Emmet, one of our Fellows, agreed to convene a study group to prepare a suitable memorandum[68] which was to stress particularly "the benefits likely to accrue to undergraduates from an unusually large senior membership" (i.e. Fellows and Senior Members).

The study group worked hard and produced drafts which were discussed and amended by the Governing Body. Then in early May 1968 came a letter to the President from the Vice Chancellor saying that again the prospect of a massive grant for a fourth women's undergraduate College had receded, so that the immediate development of Lucy Cavendish College should be planned on a graduate basis. Lucy Cavendish accepted this situation, but stated explicitly again that its ultimate aim was to take undergraduates. There the matter rested for nearly a year.

Though talk of another undergraduate College had died down, a new development in the University appeared in 1968. This was the introduction of Education into the list of subjects taught in the Cambridge Tripos Examinations and a new degree, to be known as Bachelor of Education (B.Ed.), was established. Those eligible to read for this degree were students who had become suitably qualified by three years' work in a College of Education attached to the Cambridge Institute of Education. Such students were to come to Cambridge for two years to work for the second half of the University course in Education. (Reporter 1967/8, p. 1084.) The University hoped that the Cambridge Colleges would accept such students among their members and Lucy Cavendish at once agreed that it would offer to admit and look after some of the candidates.

By this time, mid-1968, the President had been invited to attend, as an Observer, the meetings of the Colleges' Committee, where all the Heads of Houses, or their representatives, discussed current affairs. This brought Lucy Cavendish more closely in touch with the other Colleges and so made it easier for Anna to learn and understand what they were doing and thinking.

Pleased as we were with our two houses in Northampton Street, we realised that we must start looking for larger premises if the College was to expand and take part in new developments in the University. The first place to be considered was in fact the building that is now our College House, but was then known as St. Francis House. This belonged to St. John's College and in November 1967 had recently become empty. We wrote to the Bursar of that College saying that we were interested in the property and explaining how we should like to use it "as an interim headquarters". The answer came

68 The memo was to be based on memoranda already received and be within the framework of minutes and resolutions already passed by the College and its Trustees.

that no definite decision had yet been made about its future. Westcott House was mentioned as a possibility and we also heard that the West House Hotel, where we in the old Dining Group used to have our dinners, was giving up but had a three-year lease to run. This site belonged to Caius College and there was a suggestion that we might share the house with them; they using the upper part for residential purposes and we having the large rooms and kitchen on the ground floor. At first sight this seemed most hopeful, but later investigations indicated that St. Francis House would really suit us better. By this time St. John's had agreed to the idea of letting it to us. A long period of discussions and negotiations between Bursars and agents followed and it was not until July 1969 that a lease was finally signed. The lease was initially to be for a minimum of five years and the annual rent was agreed at £700.

There was much planning and discussion in the College about how best to use these new premises, a large Victorian house previously inhabited by Franciscan Brothers. Two large rooms on the ground floor became Combination Rooms, the George Bidder Room and the West Room, while a third, which had been enlarged to form a Chapel, was to become our first Library. The first floor rooms were mainly to be used by the College Officers and the College Office, and the second floor for residential accommodation.

A Buildings Committee was set up and, together with the Steward and Bursar, worked hard to prepare and furnish the house. Many other members of the College and their friends gave much time and energy in helping in a practical way or by giving or lending furnishings. Finally, the house was ready for occupation and we moved in early in February 1970.

In May 1968 Bishop Chase announced that he proposed to retire from the Chairmanship and the Board of Trustees at the end of the current academic year. Though he said that, at well over eighty, he was too old to continue, he had been from the very beginning and throughout a most excellent Chairman and the Trustees were sad to see him go. Earlier, at the time of the Cheshunt proposals, Anna Bidder had paid a special tribute to him, thanking him for "his immense support during the months of crisis". In July of that year Margaret Bottrall, owing to pressure of work, resigned as Secretary of the Trustees, but remained a member of the Board. I was appointed to take her place and so was fortunate to serve under Bishop Chase on one or two occasions before he retired. Professor Hutchinson of St. John's College replaced him as Chairman.

(Curiously, there is a break in the Trustee minutes and it seems that no meetings took place between September 1968 and March 1969. As this was the time when both the Chairman and the Secretary changed, I fear that the new Secretary (myself) must have failed to call attention to the need to arrange a meeting.)

While negotiations over St. Francis House were proceeding, Lucy Cavendish, after consultation with the Vice-Chancellor, applied again to the University for a grant to help with running expenses. This sadly was unsuccessful, as was a request to the American Friends of Cambridge to contribute to the cost of furnishing and equipping the new premises, though they relented later. However, the Geraldine S. Cadbury Fund helped us again by sending a cheque for £500 towards the move. At the same time they promised a handsome donation of £1,500 per year for five years to establish honoraria for the President, Tutor and Bursar. This was to start in 1970 and so gave us much encouragement at the start of our life in new premises, just as their earlier grant had helped us when we first moved into Northampton Street. Other pleasant donations, for which we were also most grateful, were £500 from Miss Cadbury herself, £250 from the Cripps Foundation, and the refusal of the College Secretary[69] (then Mrs. Brown) to accept a rise in salary.

Though no action had been taken since May 1968, there was still, in early 1969, considerable discussion, particularly in the College's Committee and Tutorial Representatives, on the question of increasing the number of women in the University.[70] On 6.2.69 Lucy Cavendish sent a memorandum to the Vice-Chancellor repeating the suggestion that, if a fourth College for women was to be started, we could constitute that College. It also mentioned that the whole matter could be discussed at the forthcoming visitation in May 1969 of the University Grants Committee. However, after further consultations, it became clear that there was no enthusiasm either in the University or the UGC for a new women's College, particularly as there could be an increase in the number of women through some of the existing men's Colleges 'going mixed'. In fact in early 1969 Churchill, King's and Clare Colleges, after consultation with the women's and other undergraduate Colleges, announced their intention of admitting women, probably in 1972.

Since there seemed little likelihood of a new College for women, Lucy Cavendish, again after consultation with the Vice-Chancellor, decided to seek permission to extend the scope of our work by admitting, in addition to graduate students, a small number of 'Lucy Cavendish-type' undergraduates. We realised that this would call for amendment of the terms under which the College was recognised by the University, so we prepared a document explaining why we wanted to make this application. The paper stated that "the type of undergraduate whom we have in mind is the older woman whose career has been interrupted by family and other reasons. Our main concern is with graduates of this kind, but we have evidence that there are also women in this position who need to read for a first degree. While it is of course possible for some of these to obtain places in other women's Colleges, there are some who would benefit from the particular environment and experience

---

69 Mrs. Brown was one of the excellent secretaries with whom the College was blessed and who contributed so much to its development. Sadly Mrs. Brown died in a motor accident in July 1973.
70 See "The Future of Women in the University" by Jane Collier in Cambridge Review, 20th January 1970.

of our Society, which has a primary concern for the problems involved in resuming intellectual work after interruption." The possible number of such students was "of the order of ten a year, but we do not envisage that in the early stages the number would be likely to be as many as this". The paper continued by stating that "among our present Fellows, Calouste Gulbenkian Research Fellows and Senior Members, we have people supervising for nearly every College of the University, in a wide range of subjects including a high proportion of science subjects. We do not therefore foresee any difficulty in teaching a small number of undergraduates either from our own resources or by exchange arrangements. We hope that the opportunities we could offer would encourage potential women scientists in particular to see that interruption need not prevent them from taking up academic work." The point about science subjects was mentioned since women tended to read arts subjects and so to push the balance towards those subjects rather than help to maintain or restore the fifty-fifty ratio between arts and sciences wished for by the University.

Our application was sent to the Council of the Senate on 26.6.69 and, we were told, was carefully considered by them on more than one occasion. In a long and kindly reply the Acting Registrary[71] said that the Council regretted that they could not "recommend the University to amend the terms under which your Society is recognised". The main reason for the refusal was because it was then the intention of the University "that the number of research and other graduate students should continue to grow as the necessary funds and facilities become available, but that the number of undergraduate students should remain more or less at its present level. This policy of limiting the number of undergraduates is likely to become a firm commitment, since the University Grants Committee has informed the Council that future grants to the University will be based on the assumption that there will be no substantial increase in the number of undergraduate students." Another reason was that if Lucy Cavendish were to be allowed to admit undergraduates, similar requests might be made by the other graduate societies and "the cumulative effect of such a development could add considerably to the University's difficulties in effectively implementing its policy on student numbers".

However, a suggestion was made, but not carried further, that Lucy Cavendish might like to consider following a procedure then adopted by St. Edmund's House and the Theological Colleges, whereby they selected undergraduates to read University courses, though the undergraduates were actually matriculated by one of the other Colleges. Before considering future action, we gained confirmation from our College Solicitor (Miss Barr) that she considered that the objects stated in our Trust were quite wide enough to include undergraduates as well as graduates amongst our membership. No

71 Dr.Wild and the letter was dated 30.7.1969.

further mention of undergraduates appears in the minutes of meetings until January 1970.

During the summer of 1969 Anna Bidder informed the Chairman of the Trustees (then Professor Hutchinson) that, on her doctor's orders, she would not be able to accept re-appointment as President when her present period of tenure ended in October 1970. This was reported to meetings of the Trustees and of the Governing Body and all present on both occasions expressed deep regret. They were not surprised, however, for she had asked to be allowed to retire much earlier. The Chairman then wrote to the Vice-President, Margaret Braithwaite, inviting her to discuss the future Presidency with the Governing Body and to send a nomination to the Trustees by 1st April 1970. He pointed out that though the Trust Deed stated that the Trustees should appoint the President, it was their wish to do so on the nomination of the Governing Body.

Anna Bidder then went to the USA lecturing for the rest of the Summer of 1969 and a Continuity Group was set up to deputize for her in her absence. During this time I applied for, and was granted, leave of absence during the Lent Term 1970, to continue work on the Sirenia, this time in Ceylon. Margaret Bottrall kindly agreed to act as Secretary to the Trustees and Natasha Squire, who had been appointed Assistant Tutor, to look after tutorial affairs while I was away.

Suddenly at the end of 1969 there was a reversal of Government policy on student numbers. Instead of the former strict limitation on the number of undergraduates to be admitted, there was now likely to be need for a large increase. It seems that the Department of Education and Science had found reason to revise its forecasts and now suggested that "the number of student places in Universities might need to rise from approximately 225,000 (at that time) to 450,000 by 1981" (Reporter 1969/70, pp. 647 & 1072). The Universities were consulted and Cambridge replied that "in these changed circumstances the Council think that the aim of the University should be to raise the number of students in Cambridge to, possibly, 13,500 (from approximately 10,500). The achievement of this aim would be dependent on the University being able, in consultation with the Colleges, to find a solution to the problem of accommodation." The subject was discussed by the Colleges' Committee and at that meeting our President said, "Speaking as the representative of the smallest institution here, I should like to say that Lucy Cavendish has always wished to take undergraduates. Recently we sought permission to take a small number of mature undergraduates . . . I am confident that, provided we had the necessary facilities, Lucy Cavendish would be willing by 1981 to take a substantial number of women undergraduates, both mature students and those of normal age." When Anna Bidder reported the discussion, the Governing Body "unanimously welcomed the President's initiative . . . " and at once agreed to start planning, so that when the time came for the Council of the Senate to consult with the Colleges, Lucy Cavendish would have ready a programme for an intake of undergraduates.

With the agreement of the Trustees, the President wrote to the Registrary in May 1970 informing him that "Investigations are now actively being made into the teaching potential of our Society, the possible ways of accommodating an increase of students, and the financial implications involved. It is hoped to have proposals ready to lay before the Council of the Senate if and when the decision be made to accept an increase in numbers in the University. These proposals will show why this Society wishes to be considered as the nucleus for an increase in women students in Cambridge, both graduates and undergraduates."

In July we received a long letter from the Chairman of the Standing Joint Committee on Student Numbers[72] explaining the general position and asking each College to forecast as far as possible the maximum number of students in various categories it could contain by 1976/77. We replied that our figures must be guesses as we had insufficient data to predict trends, but that a total of 150 women, 50 of them undergraduates, would be a possibility.[73] Since the latest date for the Colleges to reply was not until 31st October, it seemed best not to send to the Council of the Senate the documents about taking undergraduates which we had been so busy in preparing, but to wait till there was more information from the Government. So there was no further progress in this direction during the last two months of Anna Bidder's Presidency.

Throughout this era the Senior Members continued to rise in importance. They were consulted on all decisions of the development of the College, they contributed a large part of our teaching strength and they contained a high proportion of scientists. In May 1969 they agreed to "support a proposal for having a limited number of mature undergraduates at the present time, provided that this does not permanently define the nature of the intake of the College". They also asked that their Chairman or Vice-Chairman should attend Governing Body meetings in order to keep the Senior Members in closer touch with the affairs of the College. This, the Governing Body said, involved fundamental principles of constitution and needed further thought and discussion. Though the effects of the student unrest of 1968/69 were fortunately little felt in the College, the idea of participation was much in the air throughout the University. It was the time of a student occupation of the Senate House, and the setting up of a Consultative Committee on Participation of Junior Members in the Educational Business of the University (Reporter 1968/69, pp.954 & 973).

Another subject of interest in the College was the idea of Fellowships sponsored by industry. Though enquiries were made and there seemed to be some hopeful responses, the scheme did not come to fruition.[74] It may well

72 Sir Gordon Sutherland.
73 We added that efforts would be made to increase the proportion of scientists.
74 Joan Holgate and Marie Lawrence made enquiries, including ICI and Marks and Spencer.

have been too early in the life of the College.

A more difficult subject, and one which raised considerable emotion, was the question of the Chapel. Mention of this first came, in July 1969, in a long memorandum from one of the research students[75] proposing that the existing former Franciscan Chapel should be retained and used for worship. This was followed in March 1970 by a suggestion[76] that a questionnaire should be sent to all members of the College "to ascertain the extent of interest in the idea of converting the former *small side chapel* into a place for prayer, meditation and worship, available for use by people of all denominations". The results of the questionnaire[77] were studied by Anna Bidder who then "offered on a personal basis, to form a working party to study this problem by methods long established in the Society of Friends". Meanwhile, as a temporary measure, the side chapel was separated from the main room by a curtain and kept as a Quiet Room. The Quiet Room remained for several years but was gradually absorbed into the Library which was established in the former Chapel. Final decisions on how the rest of the rooms of the College should be used were to be left until we had lived and worked in the house for a year. One of the first floor rooms housed, until 1976, the Crystal Data Centre under the leadership of one of our Fellows, Dr. Olga Kennard.[78] The garden was large and attractive and was probably the first College garden to have its lawn mown by guinea pigs.

Six months after Anna Bidder announced her forthcoming retirement, thought was given as to how a new President should be chosen. In January 1970 the Vice President, Margaret Braithwaite, circulated a confidential memorandum suggesting a procedure. This contained very detailed proposals, made after considerable discussion with members of other Colleges and was "deliberately designed, with the aid of a good deal of advice, to create a precedent for subsequent Lucy Cavendish Presidential elections, as well as this one". After some small amendments by the Governing Body and considerable discussion, this procedure was accepted and implemented. As I was happily working in Ceylon at that time, and naturally took no part in the election of my own successor in 1979, I have no personal experience of such procedures and elections. All I knew was that one day a telegram arrived at Peradenya University asking if I was willing to be nominated for election. I accepted, with considerable trepidation, at once, but was grateful to the Fellows who gave me time after my return to Cambridge in which to speak with some of the Trustees and the officers of the College before confirming my acceptance. This done, voting was on 29th April and on 1st May the Trustees were told that "the Governing Body of Fellows had unanimously

75 Ruth McQuillan.
76 From Margaret Bottrall and Amy Clarke.
77 The results were described in a memo from Anna Bidder, circular no.141/670.
78 The North Room was once, at the request of Dr.Kennard, used by the Undergraduate Jewish Students on 25th April 1970 for Passover which fell in Full Term.

elected Cicely Kate Bertram, MA, PhD, Fellow and Tutor, as President from 1st October 1970, subject to appointment by the Trustees". The Trustees thereupon appointed me.

Soon after the election I was appointed a Trustee and my place as Secretary of the Trustees was taken by the Bursar, Joyce Linfoot. Two co-Tutors, Natasha Squire and Marie Lawrence, were elected. This happened at a time when two of the first six B.Ed. students given conditional admission to Lucy Cavendish had obtained the necessary qualifications for acceptance. It was generally agreed that the stage had been reached when the administration of the College would best be carried out by the officers and that there was no longer need to have a special officer as Secretary to the Governing Body. Further small honoraria, in addition to those made possible by the kindness of the Cadbury Fund, were agreed for the College officers.

In June 1970 we received, with great gratitude, a gift of £5,000 for corporate capital. This was the first of a long series of handsome donations from St. John's College, whose generosity has contributed much to our success. On the last day of September 1970 Anna Bidder presided at a Governing Body meeting for the last time. The meeting was held in the George Bidder Room which then contained a fine portrait of her, painted by Brenda Moore in 1968, as well as one of her father. These show our first benefactor and our first President. After the main business the Vice-President took the Chair and the retiring President was elected an Honorary Fellow. Following the meeting there was a brief formal ceremony in which I, as the new President, was installed.

The evening finished with a party given by the Senior Members in honour of Anna Bidder, and we were all conscious of how much we owed to her. She had led us through the long and difficult process of gaining University recognition, presided over us as we developed into a Graduate College with a special function, and brought it to the brink of expanding its scope to include undergraduates. All this she had done, but at some cost to her scientific work. For both her success and her sacrifice we were all deeply grateful.

3.   1970–1979.
Admissions for First Degrees

When I became President the question of whether or not Lucy Cavendish was to be allowed to admit undergraduates as well as graduate students was still under discussion in the University. By December 1970 the Colleges jointly had said that they would be able by 1976/77 to admit and accommodate 1,350 additional students, a figure agreed with the University Grants

Committee. Lucy Cavendish, still hoping for a share in this increase, was delighted to hear that the Council of the Senate had set up a special committee to consider our application to take some undergraduates. After investigating our finances the Council's Committee published its report in May 1971 (Reporter 1970/71,p.784). This recommended that the University should amend its Statute H.IV so that Approved Societies were no longer to be restricted to graduates only. It also proposed that the regulations for Lucy Cavendish should be amended so as to allow us to admit up to a total of 50 students reading for first degrees. These were to be either not less than 25 years of age or entitled to be approved as Affiliated Students (i.e. graduate students taking an undergraduate degree in two years). The report also mentioned that the Committee had considered the possible alternative of recommending that Lucy Cavendish should be recognised as an Approved Foundation, but had decided that we had not yet sufficient resources in the form of endowment, land and buildings to justify that status. It is interesting to note, however, that the possibility of our being an Approved Foundation was considered at such an early date. The recommendations were accepted and the way was now clear for us to intensify our plans and preparations for our first undergraduates who were to be admitted in October 1972. This new expansion was particularly welcome at a time when the Science Research Council and other grant-giving bodies were about to cut down the number or duration of grants available to research students. This, together with the fact that some of the men's Colleges were about to admit women, could seriously affect our intake of these graduate students.

However, in October 1970, the first members of a new category of students arrived which, for eight years, increased our student numbers considerably. These were the women wishing to read for the degree of Bachelor of Education (see p.). Though we had offered places to six applicants in this category, in fact only two passed the necessary University qualification. We welcomed them joyfully and they did us much credit, one of them gaining a Class I degree at the end of the academic year.[74] This feat may have made Lucy Cavendish the only College in Cambridge to have 50% of its students achieving first class marks in the Tripos examinations in any one year! They were also very helpful to us in that, being of graduate student status, and yet reading for an undergraduate degree, they enabled us, and particularly the Tutors, to gain experience about University procedures concerning those reading for a first degree. The next year ten were admitted, then sixteen, and the annual intake remained at about this level until the system came to an end in 1978. Altogether the College admitted 73 of these B.Ed. students. They added much to the life and liveliness of the College and we were sorry to lose them when the system ended. The next task which awaited the Governing Body that first term of the academic year 1970/71 concerned the Senior Members.

79 Mrs.Joyce Dobbie.

The Governing Body was reminded that when the category of Senior Members was first being considered in 1966 (see p. 00), it was agreed that the College should recognise some responsibility for furthering their academic work. It was now suggested that the office of College Lecturer should be established for those of our Senior Members who were most deeply involved in teaching in other Colleges. Such an office would give the holders more standing in the University and we hoped that it would make it possible for them to qualify for an M.A. degree if they were not already Cambridge graduates, but this was not to be. It was also hoped that the office would 'hold' these teaching Senior Members until our own undergraduates arrived. We feared that we might lose them to other Colleges with the result that our teaching strength could be seriously weakened. The proposal to establish the office of College Lecturer was accepted and welcomed by both the Trustees and the Governing Body. At first the office was to be non-stipendiary, but a generous donation from Gonville and Caius College[80] of £1,000 per annum for five years provided small emoluments for the holders and in April 1971 seven College Lecturers[81] were appointed from among 13 applicants.

The Trustees, being essentially responsible for the College's finances, spent much of their meetings discussing financial policy and whether the time was ripe for planning further Appeals. Our total assets at that time amounted to about £15,000 of which £10,000 had been designated as corporate capital which meant that it could not be used for recurrent expenses[82].

With the coming expansion of numbers the need for further buildings had become very evident. The idea of a dining hall had been in our minds for some while and we had amused ourselves making unconventional designs. The first real suggestion, however, came when the Vice-President, Margaret Braithwaite, told the Trustees that she had discussed the subject with Mr. John Walker of the Rugby Cement Company. She had explained to him that the College needed a hall where all the members could meet together, but that as yet we had little money and no definite permanent home. Under these circumstances the hall should be as inexpensive as possible and capable of translocation if we were ever to move. Mr. Walker had been interested in the idea and believed that, through his contacts in industry, a steel-framed demountable building could be produced and that its major components might be contributed by the manufacturers as an advertisement for modern constructional methods.

Margaret Braithwaite had also talked with Mr. John Meunier of the Cambridge University School of Architecture who seemed interested in such a project and would be prepared to act as architect. As an exercise for some

---

80 Caius also gave us £400 a year for 5 years to provide free dinners for Fellows.
81 These were Helen Alderson, Jane Collier, Hilda Davidson, Eva Mason, Janet Moore, Doris Thoday and Mindele Treip.
82 These sums included £2,000 from Anna Bidder and for furnishing £2,000 from the American Friends of Cambridge University.

of his students he had asked them to visit the site and prepare possible schemes. Some of these were highly original.

After discussion with the Trustees and particularly with Mr. Walker, Mr. Meunier produced a feasibility study and later some plans. From this time on, and for two years, the proposed dining hall, its lay-out, siting, size, expenses and how to find the necessary funds to build it, were discussed at every level. Its inclusion in any Appeal document was agreed and we had even obtained planning permission for it to be on the eastern border of the College garden. Then suddenly, in July 1973, the whole idea was shelved as a result of the generous gift of a neighbouring house.

With increasing numbers the need for residential accommodation was acute, especially as we had to return to Magdalene College in September 1976 the two houses in Northampton Street which had been accommodating about eight of our students since we moved to Lady Margaret Road in 1970. The Bursar was actively seeking suitable houses. During her search a variety of possibilities was considered. These included a large house in Grange Road which could offer furnished accommodation, some nearby almshouses, a house in Madingley road, as well as Strathaird, Barrmore and The Gables in Lady Margaret Road, the road in which the College House is situated. The Bursar, with the support of a Committee, investigated all these and it became apparent that Strathaird and Barrmore were easily the most suitable. Not only were they of about the same date and style as the College House, they were in the same row and all stood on leasehold land belonging to St. John's College.[83]

As early as November 1971 Mrs. Margot Bulman, the owner of Strathaird, wrote confidentially to me as President suggesting that she would like to help the College by offering us that house when she and Professor Oliver Bulman were able to move to a smaller house nearby, then lived in by her mother, Mrs. Fearnsides. This offer was of immense generosity since they planned to hand over the house to Lucy Cavendish as a gift, to pay the rates until we moved in, to repair the roof and to ask in return only for up to 10 years' free occupancy for their own use should this be necessary. The ground lease was then bought by the College for £10,000, which Mrs. Bulman and her mother then gave us as an additional donation.

A year later, in May 1973, Mrs. Fearnsides died and the Bulmans moved into her house in Mount Pleasant, leaving Strathaird free for the College. By great efforts on the part of many people it was possible for the first five students to move in for the Michaelmas Term. Mrs. Bulman added to her already outstanding benefaction by leaving furniture for their rooms and for a Fellows' drawing room. She also left behind many treasures so that the house should continue to look, as she said, "civilised".

Plans for enlarging the kitchen were already being prepared by Beryl Green, then an architectural research student of the College. The final plan involved

83 Much thought was also given to The Gables, across the road, but it was found not to be in good enough condition.

covering over an enclosed yard which would provide the kitchen space likely to be needed to cook for the whole College for the foreseeable future. It could supply food either to a new dining hall built alongside or to a dining room formed from two of the adjoining downstairs rooms. The dining room in the house was chosen and the schemes for building a new dining hall were dropped. Later the cost of the construction of the new kitchen was contributed by the Pilgrim Trust and its equipment was given by the American Friends of Cambridge University.

While we were making plans for Strathaird, we heard in February 1972 that the occupant of Barrmore[84] had died. As this house lay between the College House and Strathaird, we were extremely interested in what would happen to it. However, it seemed that the owner was not considering any immediate sale. Fortunately, he did agree to our renting two flats in the house which was helpful.

Now that it seemed probable that this region could become our home for some time, we asked St. John's College how long we could continue to rent the College House from them. The answer was that we could stay there anyhow until 1996 when the ground lease came to an end.

In March 1974 we heard that a sale of Barrmore was being proposed. After discussion and investigation, we made a preliminary offer which was rejected. The next news was that a sale by auction was planned and we went through a tense period fearing that the house would be sold for more than we could afford. There were rumours that bids of the order of £20,000 were in the air. Then came the news that an application for planning permission for change of use of Barrmore had been made on behalf of the Transcendental Meditationists. We at once sent an objection since the whole of the area was designated for collegiate use only. Nothing more was heard on that subject. Eventually, early in 1975, emboldened by some handsome donations, the very high interest rates then prevalent, and a rise in share prices, the Trustees authorised the raising of our bid to £21,000. This was accepted and Barrmore became ours. Now it really did look as though we were becoming established in Lady Margaret Road which led us to consider the possibility of buying from St. John's the freehold of the three houses. This was important, not only in the long term, but also because it became clear that grant-giving bodies were loath to give help for buildings to those who did not own their land. Fortunately St. John's, in June 1975, agreed in principle to sell us the freeholds of the property we then occupied, provided that it was for collegiate use only. Discussions over price were started and in February 1976 the Bursar was authorised to make plans to purchase the three freeholds in the coming summer. The Trustees wished, however, before any action was taken, to hear the views of the Fellows of Lucy Cavendish and at a Joint Meeting with the Governing Body, "there was general approval of the Trustees' proposal and

84 Occupant was Miss Wilkinson who died in February 1972. Owner was Dr.Crick.

they and the Bursar were congratulated by the Fellows on making the purchase of the freeholds possible". At the beginning of September, the purchase was completed at a price of £80,000. This meant that we now owned three large Victorian houses with their attractive gardens, forming altogether a site of 2.7 acres. The Wolfson Trust[85] sent us a welcome cheque for £10,000 to help with the purchase.

I should like here to pay a personal tribute to the Bursar, Joyce Linfoot. She was throughout the most determined advocate for the purchase of the freeholds and carried it out with great skill. This view was also expressed by others, one of whom wrote to her saying, "purchasing the freeholds must have justified itself many times over: the benefits have emerged in all kinds of ways. The wisdom of doing this owes much to your foresight and financial management".

In October 1972, after so many years of negotiating and waiting, we were able to welcome our first intake of undergraduates. There were 20 of them, varying in age from 25 to 36, thus qualifying as mature students and meeting the University requirements of Statute H. They brought a great deal of liveliness to the College, coming from diverse backgrounds and all with interesting post-school experience. Their previous occupations were varied and included secretaries, housewives, teachers and an actress.

The College was particularly interested to discover how these mature, would-be undergraduates had learnt about the College, because the UCCA handbook[86] had as yet no information. Most came because of personal contacts, but others resulted from publicity about the College in newspaper articles or on radio. One of them was ironing in an army station in Germany when she heard of the College in Woman's Hour. She determined to apply for admission as soon as she was posted back to England.

The new undergraduates settled well into Cambridge life. The College had set up an organisation of Tutors and Directors of Studies which followed very closely the system in other Colleges. The aim was to make Lucy Cavendish undergraduates different from others only in the matter of age. The two Tutors, Marie Lawrence and Natasha Squire, with great skill and with help and encouragement from their colleagues in other Colleges made the system work well. The admission process was different for mature students, and interviewers had to discover if aspiring undergraduates had, for example, considered carefully what provisions they would make for family illness and other difficulties likely to arise from having domestic responsibilities. It would have been no kindness to applicants to admit them unless they had given considerable thought to these potential problems.

85 The Wolfson Trust, with whom we were in contact, was kept informed of the position and in May 1976 a formal application was sent to them asking for help with the purchase. Sadly the Director told us with deep regret that our request was not successful. However they later repented to some extent.
86 UCCA stands for Universities Central Council for Admissions.

English was the most popular choice of subject among the 12 subjects chosen by the first intake. There was much speculation about how well our mature students would do in University examinations. One view was that the results would be good because of the undoubtedly high motivation of mature students. They had indeed to be well motivated to give up well-paid jobs, or undertake academic work despite domestic responsibilities. The opposing view was that mature students would be out of practice at reading and writing essays and, being older, would learn more slowly and have less retentive memories than 18-year-olds. In fact their results compared quite favourably with those of undergraduates in general, being about average.

The increase in numbers, coming with the admission of undergraduates, meant that many changes had to be made. First the Library had to be developed. The first mention of a Library appeared in the Governing Body minutes in July 1971 when the College Lecturers were asked to establish one and to investigate ways of stocking it so that it could be useful to B.Eds. and future undergraduates. Soon a Library Committee was formed and in February 1972 a Librarian, Ursula Lyons, was appointed. The first Library was set up in a ground floor room in the College House where it remained for nearly four years.

1975 saw a number of changes. Harriet Crawford was appointed Librarian, together with Phyllis Giles and Julie Larter as fellow Librarians, and a panel of representatives from all sections of the College. Overnight borrowing was instituted on a trial basis. In 1976, as a result of grants from the Pilgrim Trust and the Colleges' Library Fund, the Library was moved in wheelbarrows across to two newly-converted rooms in Barrmore, where it still remains. Shelving of a "murderous dark green" was borrowed from New Hall on long loan and the rearrangement was completed by the beginning of the Michaelmas Term. In 1977 the Library panel became a sub-committee of the Governing Body and the Librarian became an Official Fellow, a new category of Fellowship, formed the previous year. A grant in 1978 from the Fairway Trust enabled us to replace the steel shelving with more modern Swedish shelves which proved much more amenable.

During the next eight years the Library was to expand to something in the region of 7,000 volumes, with annual borrowing of more than 1,000 books. It runs largely on a trust basis and the losses have been satisfactorily low. A modified Dewey catalogue system is used and a borrowers' register. Major donations in cash and kind have been received from many sources.

Early in 1971 the question of a crest and armorial bearings arose when a kindly donor,[87] who then wished to remain anonymous, offered the necessary grant fee. The College gladly accepted this offer and invited Mr. C.W. Scott-

---

87 The generous donor is now allowing me to give her name: Mrs. Margaret Mayne, a member of the Roll of the College.

Giles, Fitzalan Pursuivant of Arms Extraordinary,[88] to prepare a design. He produced a proposal and put us in touch with the Richmond Herald of Arms who prepared a suitable Memorial. The Vice-President and I much enjoyed a visit to see him at the College of Arms where we learned about the meaning of crests and badges and that corporations, whether male, female or mixed, are able to use a crest. Both the drawings and Memorial were generally accepted and it seemed that all would go well. However, there was a delay caused by a legal difficulty inasmuch as a grant could not be made to Trustees since they are not a corporate body. Fortunately it seemed that the University, if they were willing, could receive it on our behalf. This they did and the Garter King of Arms finally approved the grant at the end of 1973. The shield depicts a waterlily, chosen as a floral emblem suited to a riverside situation, a buck's head from the arms of the Cavendish family, and a scallop shell from the heraldry of the Lytteltons. The crest consists of a Nautilus shell, a marine animal studied by Anna Bidder, and three estoiles or 'lights' alluding to the name Lucy[89]. The grant gave, and continues to give, much pleasure to the members of the College. Twelve years later the shield was flown on a banner for the first time when H.R.H. the Duke of Edinburgh, as the College's Visitor, came to the College in 1985.

The most urgent need of the College at the time when our undergraduate numbers had come up to their full strength was the improvement and extension of residential accommodation. The first alterations to our buildings were the formation of the kitchen and dining room in Strathaird already mentioned (see p.). At the end of 1974 there were further improvements in this house. One was the fitting of an accoustic ceiling to the dining room, which greatly reduced the noise level at meal times. Another was the glassing-in of the verandah outside to form a bar, a valuable addition. A solar panel was installed on the roof above the kitchen, making us the first College in Cambridge to use the sun to heat water. The solar heater was put in partly to measure how much heat it could provide on that particular site, as a guide to the feasibility of using solar energy in a future building. It was also good for publicity at a time when we were planning an Appeal. It was paid for from the President's Fund, a delightful fund given anonymously in October 1970, with the instruction that it was to be used at the discretion of the President only. A separate kitchen was also provided, for the students. All these and later improvements were designed and largely carried out by Beryl Green, who by then had offered to look after the College buildings on a voluntary basis and had been appointed Buildings Advisory Officer in 1975.

The next improvements were to Barrmore in July 1975 where, as already mentioned, a ground floor flat was converted into the new Library. Also a small coach house was altered to form two supervision rooms. Some years

88 He was the brother of one of our Fellows, Phyllis Giles, and the Richmond Herald of Arms was then Mr.J.P.Brooke Little.
89 See "The Cambridge Armorial", 1985, p.126.

later, in 1978, additional rooms were cleverly carved out of the roof spaces in both Barrmore and the College House.[90]

For all these and other developments the College needed funds. Student fees and interest on capital covered the main running costs, but money for building and endowment had to be sought from outside. Before describing our first widespread Appeal, perhaps it would be useful to give a brief summary of the financial history of the College up to 1970.

When it first sought recognition by the University, Lucy Cavendish had a capital sum of £3,000. During 1966 it collected about £4,500 gross, mostly in covenants subscribed by its members and their friends. At the same time it appealed to the other Cambridge Colleges to help with initial development, and received donations amounting to about £4,000. In 1967 it appealed to M.A.s resident in Cambridge for monies to be used particularly in building up the corporate life of the College when the new category of Senior Membership was being established. This Appeal produced, again mostly in covenants, a further sum of the order of £4,000. In this year the Barrow and Geraldine S. Cadbury Trust ganted £500 per year for three years.

Next came two earmarked benefactions; one in 1967 of £5,000 per year for three years from the Calouste Gulbenkian Foundation for research awards (see p.) and the other in 1970 of £1,500, later raised to £1,750, per year for five years from the Cadbury Trust mentioned above for honoraria for certain College Officers (see p.). Also in 1970 St. John's College made a donation of £5,000 to be designated as corporate capital. This was followed in subsequent years by three more gifts of £5,000, then in increasing amounts making a total of £95,000 by 1979. These handsome gifts made St. John's our greatest benefactor and we were profoundly grateful. (See Appendix VII for inflation table.)

As a first step towards a wide appeal we decided in 1971 again to approach other Cambridge Colleges asking for a nucleus of support. I therefore visited the Heads of most of the wealthier Colleges to tell them about our activities, our progress and the need for our forthcoming Appeal. This turned out to be a very pleasant task as they all seemed sympathetic to our aims and interested in our development. The result was pleasing: a total of £12,000 was received or promised from nine Colleges (Clare, Corpus Christi, Churchill, Emmanuel, Jesus, King's, Queens', Trinity & Peterhouse, many of which gave us further donations later in addition to St. John's already mentioned).

During these visits I was often asked whether we received help from the Colleges Fund: a fund set up in June 1966 (Reporter, 1965/66, p. 1,048) for which the richer Colleges were taxed for the benefit of the University and of some of the poorer Colleges. I had to explain that, as an Approved Society, we were not eligible to apply to this source, but that any money given us

90 We received a gift of £10,000 towards the cost of conversion of Barrmore and donations from 55 manufacturing firms contributed to the cost of furnishing.

by a College would be taken into account by the University when assessing its contribution to the Fund.

The Colleges Fund was discussed many times in our Trustee meetings and twice we made formal requests that Lucy Cavendish should be able to apply for a grant. The first was early in 1973 when we asked whether our position could be reconsidered now that we were doing a considerable amount of teaching for the University and were admitting undergraduates. The second, made jointly with Hughes Hall, was in 1975 when we asked specifically for Statute GII of the University to be amended so as to allow Approved Societies to become eligible for a grant. Neither request was successful: it is not until the status of Approved Foundation is reached that it becomes possible to gain help from the Colleges Fund.

Having secured a nucleus of support from the Cambridge Colleges, we now needed some general publicity. Most generously Dr. E.J. Lindgren (a Founding Fellow), in collaboration with her friend, Miss Mary E. Wood, offered to give a party in London to introduce the Fellows and Honorary Fellows of Lucy Cavendish to a wide range of influential people, including Members of Parliament, to take place in the House of Commons with Dame Irene Ward as Sponsor. Arrangements were well advanced when a re-organisation of the kitchens and car park at Westminster caused the cancellation of all reservations. Rooms in the English Speaking Union were quickly substituted and the event took place there on 16th November 1972. Though sad in some ways, this change of venue had the advantage that we could display our plans for the Appeal whereas this would have been impossible in the House of Commons where there are strict limitations on the promotion by publication of particular interests. About 150 guests were invited and about 70 attended including 20 Fellows and Trustees.[91] Unfortunately a three-line Whip at the last minute prevented some Members of the House appearing. It was a happy and successful occasion which "splendidly achieved the object of making the College more widely known", and lifted it out of the local and into the national scene. Grateful thanks were given to Dr. Lindgren and to Miss Wood, who then accepted Honorary Membership of the College and always joined us at the last dinner of the academic year in Cambridge.

A special sheet, dated October 1972, was prepared for this party giving a brief description of the College and its activities. Soon a longer and more detailed prospectus was planned with an account of its aims, history, premises, achievements, finances and future growth. This passed through many drafts, all open to comment by all the Fellows, and strong views were held even on the colour of the cover. Eventually it was ready for printing in 1975 and became known as the Purple Booklet. It was designed for anyone who might be, or could be, interested in the College and for inclusion in any future Appeal literature.

91 Mr.Edward Heath was among those who wrote regretting that he was unable to accept the invitation. His letter is in the College.

The next question was how best to run the Appeal: whether to employ a professional fund-raiser or to try and do it ourselves. We sought the advice of the Secretary of the Cadbury Trust[92] knowing that he was used to receiving and evaluating appeals. His view was that if you are trying to do something new it is important "not to let anyone get between you and your image" and that, in such cases, it was wiser to appoint someone from within the organisation to run the Appeal rather than an outside firm. With this in mind we decided to embark on a consultancy service offered by Craigmyle & Co. as a compromise.[93] The consultant appointed came on four occasions bringing with him quantities of lists of names and other helpful information. At a time when there was great activity in the College with many meetings and working parties all considering the Appeal, it was a help to me personally to be able to discuss some of their proposals with an expert and hear his assessment of their value.

Meanwhile preparation of the necessary Appeal documents went ahead and the target to cover the development of the College for the next few years was set at £500,000. The Governing Body confirmed its view that, for the foreseeable future, Lucy Cavendish should continue to be primarily for mature women and to aim at "helping women returners, late starters and career changers". Additionally a working party convened by the Vice-President, Margaret Braithwaite, proposed that a centre should be set up within the College to give practical help to its members in establishing their careers. The Trustees were sympathetic to the idea, but decided that this should not be included in the Appeal, though it did arise again at a later date (see p. 00).

During February 1975 Mr. Anthony Wilson, Secretary of the Cadbury Trust, came to the College and talked informally with some of the officers, including the Tutors and the Buildings Advisory Officer. The main topics discussed were the need for further honoraria and the mechanics of running an Appeal. A short while later, in response to a telephone call from Mr. Wilson, I, helped by the Bursar, sent a formal letter to the Cadbury Trust. This asked for a further grant, since their earlier one had just ended, to enable officers' payments to be continued and to help with the organisation of the Appeal. A copy of my letter was considered by the Lucy Cavendish Trustees at their meeting on 4th March and, while the President and Bursar withdrew, confirmed the figures suggested. On 19th March we received a

92 Mr.Anthony Wilson.
93 We had, in April 1973, made contact with the firm Richard Meurice and Co. whose representative (Col.Cable) came to the College and I visited the Company office. While considering what they could offer an unexpected letter arrived from Craigmyle and Co. enclosing a description of a consultancy service as an alternative to a fund raiser. One of the Directors (Mr.Hamilton) came to see us and explained that a member of the company should visit the College and advise on procedures and suggest ways of enlarging our constituency which was small, having as yet but few past members to call upon. The consultant appointed (Mr.R.O.Davis) visited on four occasions between 7.5.74 and 7.11.75 bringing lists of women directors, of companies which employed women, and of grant-giving bodies interested in women's education.

letter stating that the Trustees of the Cadbury Trust were prepared to help us again. A sum of £9,000 a year for three years was offered towards increased staffing costs for both administration and in connection with an Appeal. Further, the letter explained that in considering our application "special attention was paid to the case for having a salary for the Development Officer. The Trustees (of the Cadbury Trust) agreed that such a full-time post would appear to be the best means of attracting the finance which the College needs for its survival and continued expansion." A later letter explained there was unlikely to be an extension of this grant beyond the three years originally envisaged.

This handsome donation was reported to the Governing Body of Lucy Cavendish on 30th April 1975 and accepted with grateful thanks. On 22nd May our Trustees set up a Committee[94] to consider the appointment of a full-time Development Officer and the remuneration of the College Officers and others involved with fund-raising.

On 19th June the Trustees accepted the recommendations of this Committee and appointed Beryl Green as Development Officer for a year in the first instance with a salary of £3,000. She was chosen particularly as she had experience of running an appeal for a school and was already involved in development work on a voluntary basis in her capacity as Buildings Advisory Officer. Two other special appointments were that Margaret Braithwaite was to become Pro-President with responsibility for planning, and Mary Hamer (a Senior Member with experience of publicity) as Information Officer. Apart from these new Officers and a grant for Appeal expenses, the rest of the Cadbury grant was to be used to augment the honoraria of the existing College Officers. These appointments and arrangements were all of an ad hoc nature and co-terminous with the Cadbury donation.

The special Officers were to be responsible to a Development Committee consisting of the Chairman of Trustees, the President, Bursar, one of the Tutors, a student representative and any other member subsequently appointed. These later included Harriet Crawford (Librarian) and Eileen Aldworth (Chairman of Senior Members). The Committee was to report to the Trustees, to meet regularly and from time to time with the Governing Body. These arrangements were also to be co-terminous with the Cadbury grant. On 15th July, at its first meeting since May, the Governing Body expressed its "concern that it was not informed of these developments at an earlier stage". It also asked for a clearer definition of the functions of the Development Committee and that this Committee should report regularly to the Governing Body as well as to the Trustees. This concern was justified and, with hind-sight, I much regret that extra meetings were not called, unpopular as these are in the Long Vacation, so that the Fellows could have been more involved. I, and perhaps some of the other Trustees also, had

94 Committee consisted of Mrs.Bottrall, Prof.Hutchinson and Dr. Willson.

misjudged the extent to which the relations between the Governing Body and the Trustees was changing. For so long the Fellows had been content to leave the control of the finances and the external affairs of the College in the hands of the Trustees. The imminence of an Appeal, however, had the effect of making everyone realise that we must have a clear idea of how the College was constituted as well as how it should develop. A definitive constitution, at least in draft, as well as detailed development plans, would be needed in the preparation of an Appeal document. In both these matters the Governing Body naturally wanted to share in the making of decisions about the future.

The relationship between the Trustees and the Governing Body was the subject of discussion in many Governing Body meetings and in five Joint Meetings between July 1976 and February 1979. Throughout the Trustees insisted that they wished to hand over their responsibility to the Governing Body as soon as practicable and allowed by the terms of the Trust Deed. Meanwhile it was accepted that the two bodies had different roles and agreed that there should be maximum communication and collaboration between them. Though there was some criticism of the fact that four Fellows were members of both bodies, it was pointed out that this dual representation had been useful in the past as the main channel of communication. No changes were made and the College was particularly grateful to the 'outside' Trustees for all the time they gave to help with the Appeal in addition to their formal responsibilities.

The Development Officer, backed by the Development Committee[95], started work energetically as soon as they were appointed in June 1975. Before this date many activities, designed to collect and channel ideas, had already taken place. These included open meetings, discussion among students and Senior Members as well as among Fellows, a workshop entitled ' Recycling Womanpower'[96], and various other activities. Four working parties within the College had collected background information to be used in the preparation of the Appeal document. Their reports were summarised in December 1974 in sections entitled 'The Need', 'An Institution designed to meet it', 'Evidence for achievements of mature-age students' and 'Opportunities of Employment for the mature Woman in the Professions'.

The Development Committee worked hard, holding 15 meetings before it came to an end in March 1976. Such was the enthusiasm in the College that the membership of this committee grew rapidly and, in trying to include as

95 The appointment of a Development Officer, Development Committee, and special officers also added to the complication. These were all ad hoc appointments and had to be fitted into the existing structure of the College making further definition of responsibilities and duties necessary.

96 The Workshop was chaired by Joan Boulind, newly retired Co- Chairman of the Women's National Commission, and the main participants represented women's organizations, careers advisers, management consultants and accountancy. The reports of the Workshop are in the College.

many as possible of those wanting to belong, it became somewhat unwieldy. Nonetheless the Appeal document was ready for circulation by December 1976. The covering letter, warmly supporting the Appeal, was signed by the Vice-Chancellor of that time (Rosemary Murray) and three former Vice-Chancellors.[97] The Appeal document itself described the College, stated what it was doing, explained its aims and enclosed a 10-year development plan. This plan was designed to maintain maximum flexibility for development and yet remain viable at all stages: the priorities however were not rigid. It envisaged that the endowment required for the payment of people would be of the order of £1,750,000. This would include scholarships and bursaries for students, and salaries and grants for those involved in teaching, research and administration. Additionally endowment was needed for buildings and land and this would be about £1,000,000, including funds for conversion of existing property for residential accommodation and a Library. The 10-year plan had earlier been shown to the Registrary[98] and to the University Treasurer who thought it well set out and on an appropriate scale.

From the start of the Appeal the Development Officer was tireless in drafting innumerable letters, arranging visits to, and visitors from, companies and organising lunch parties for potential benefactors. By April 1979 she was able to report that the Appeal had raised £212,000 in gifts or promises. This sum came from 17 Cambridge Colleges, 15 Charitable Trusts, 7 Worshipful Companies, 15 Banks and Insurance Companies, 7 interested organisations and 45 firms in commerce and industry. The figure of £212,000 did not include the earlier grants from the Gulbenkian Foundation and the Cadbury Trust amounting to £33,850. At the last Joint Meeting of the Trustees and Governing Body in January 1979, tribute was paid to the Development Officer, Beryl Green, when she was "congratulated on the amount of hard work and ingenuity she had put into fund-raising, not only through the Appeal". Certainly with her skill, energy and enthusiasm she made a great contribution to the development of the College.

Returning now to the constitution of the College, the basic structure was laid down in the Trust Deed of 1965. This defined the part that should be taken by the Trustees. They had, unless they delegated some of their responsibility, to approve all expenditure, statutes and regulations, appointments, relations with persons and organisations outside the College, and any other matter they deemed relevant to their duties.

Both the Trustees and the Governing Body had always agreed that the aim of the College was that it should develop from being an Approved Society to become an Approved Foundation as soon as possible (see Appendix IV). In 1974 they began to look closely into how this could be done. It seemed that there were three criteria by which an institution wanting to take this

97 Lord Ashby, Prof. Owen Chadwick and Prof. Alex Deer.
98 Registrary was Mr.R.E.Macpherson and Treasurer was Mr.T.C.Gardner.

step was judged. First it must be academically respectable: the achievements of our Fellows, our publications and our examination results were, we believed, sufficiently good. Secondly, it must be financially viable: this was still a distant target, but our Appeal was designed to bring it nearer. Financial independence was of great importance, for the University was under no obligation to bail out an Approved Society in difficulty, whereas it was expected to give help to an Approved Foundation under such circumstances. Thirdly, an aspiring Approved Society must have a constitution written in a form suitable to meet University requirements.[99] A written constitution would also be needed to satisfy benefactors who like to know how and by whom their money is to be handled. It would also ease the government of the College as a continuing institution, since too much time is consumed if each decision has to be thrashed out afresh on each occasion.

Our first step forward was to summarise in 1975 the constitutional position as it then was. This task was ably done by Dr. Mindele Treip, then Secretary to the Constitution Committee, which contained both Trustees and members of the Governing Body, in a paper entitled 'Customs and Practices in the Government of the College, 1965–75.'[100] The next step was to seek legal advice on how to proceed. Despite his being on sabbatical leave, Mr. D.E.C. Yale, then Reader in English Legal History and the University's main adviser on College statutes, kindly agreed to help us. He explained that what the University needed was to be assured that the institution in question was governed by members of the Senate and was recognisably a College. Further he recommended that we should examine some of the most recent statutes for Cambridge Colleges and use them as a model. It chanced that at this stage I had been given sabbatical leave from January to March 1976 to go back to the sea-cows of Guyana. Since these are elusive animals I expected to have spare time and so offered to prepare a draft. The offer was accepted and I took with me copies of the statutes of New Hall, Fitzwilliam, Girton, Wolfson and Darwin Colleges. I chose those of New Hall as the prototype because they seemed the most comprehensive and they were particularly recommended by Mr. Yale. In general all the statutes were similar in principle, the main differences being in the amount of detail included. Usually I followed the most detailed since agreement on the points they included was needed before our statutes could be operated. Some of the points could later be removed to Ordinances or Regulations if so wished. Some new sections had to be added to cover our Senior Membership since this was a class of membership not occurring elsewhere among the Colleges.

On my return to Cambridge, I suggested that my draft statutes should be used as a working guide which could be modified where experience showed a need for change. This suggestion was accepted by the Governing Body and

99 From the beginning our accounts were in the form required by the University for the Colleges.
100 College circular no.51/775.

the draft became the subject of wide discussion in the College. As a result many minor amendments and improvements were made. Doubts about the position of Senior Members took us back to Mr. Yale for further legal advice. He considered that Senior Members could properly be included in the corporate body as it was not necessary for members of the corporate body to be members of the Governing Body. Therefore, by general agreement of the Trustees and Governing Body, the Senior Members were included in the statute defining the corporate body which consisted of "The President, Fellows and Senior Members" of Lucy Cavendish. Agreement was also reached that Senior Members should make the same declaration of loyalty as the Fellows when they were formally admitted to the College. In the section on the Governing Body, the power of this body to delegate was confirmed. Although there was provision for a Council, it was agreed that one was still not needed at present. The size of the Governing Body was to be limited to not more than 30 in number and should normally not exceed more than one-fifth of the total membership of the College.

During the early 1970s considerable changes and important events were occurring in the University. It was a time of student unrest in many Universities in the country and demands for student participation were widely heard. In February 1972 in Cambridge the Senate House was occupied for two days by students seeking more share in the running of the University. After this sit-in, which caused widespread shock in the University, the Council of the Senate invited Lord Devlin, then High Steward of the University, to lead an intensive enquiry. Lord Devlin accepted and made a detailed study of the whole affair and of the general administration of the University. He reported his findings and recommendations in a long and detailed paper entitled 'Report of the Sit-in in February 1972 and its Consequences' (Reporter 1972/73, Special No. 12). He had come to the conclusion that it was time for some of the existing procedures in the University to be modified so that students could take more part in its government. After much discussion the Council of the Senate prepared a report (Reporter 1972/73, p. 1,379) which included the recommendation that, as an interim measure, the President of the Cambridge Students Union and the President of the Graduate Society should be invited to attend meetings of the Council of the Senate. They were to be allowed to speak on any matter, but not to vote, and there was provision for reserved business. Later, the presence of student observers at meetings of the Council beame a regular feature and the arrangement continued.[101]

In Lucy Cavendish the first request for observers at Governing Body meetings had come from the Senior Members in 1969 (see p. 00). By May 1975 the students, too, were asking for such observers and at the first meeting of the next academic year members of both bodies were welcomed. They

101 There was also a recommendation that students should not be represented on the General or Financial Boards, nor have a vote in the Regent House.

were also present when the Governing Body met jointly with the Trustees. Later both Senior Members and students were represented as full members on the main committees of the College.

There were other important matters being discussed in the University at this time. There was the munificent gift from Mr. David Robinson of £10 million to found a new College in Cambridge. This was to be "for both male and female members of the University" (Reporter, 1973/74, pp. 446, 524 & 606). It became Robinson College and admitted its first students in 1977 (see Appendix III). In 1974 the General Board published a lengthy, detailed and wide-ranging report on the long-term development of the University (Reporter 1974/75, p.542). In particular it recommended that the University, both for its own good and for that of the city, should not continue to grow in numbers and should remain in a "steady-state" with about 14,000 students.[102] This proposed limitation of numbers of students in the future caused uncertainties for the Colleges, particularly in connection with residential accommodation. Despite the uncertainties we, in Lucy Cavendish, thought that an increase in our small number of students was of such importance to our financial viability and proper development, that in 1977 we asked to be allowed to increase our number of undergraduates in residence from 50 to 80 over the next three years. Sadly, but as we had feared, the Council of the Senate told us that all decisions on student numbers were being deferred for a year. In fact no increase had by 1985 been allowed in spite of later requests. One of these, in the summer of 1978, asked if, as numbers of graduate students was falling and the supply of B.Eds. finishing, an increase of undergraduates could then be allowed. This was also unsuccessful, but the possibility of increasing the number of our graduate students by admitting some clinical medical students was mentioned.

By this time the students of Lucy Cavendish were taking an active part in many spheres of College and University life. Within the College pantomimes were written and performed, concerts played and Judo courses arranged. The small numbers of undergraduates meant that any particular activity depended on the number of enthusiastic and willing participants. Some years music was 'in', others years, acting. In the University our students were already active in many societies and sports, including rowing. They also made the College a focus of activity for other mature students in the University. Special meetings, dinners and parties brought mature students, rather rare people in many Colleges, to Lucy Cavendish and made the College better known among other members of the University.

Towards the end of 1977 it was clear that many changes in the College were about to occur. The latest grant from the Cadbury Trust, made in 1970, covering most of the Appeal administration and the honoraria of the College

102 The Report also contained the view that the ratio between those reading Science and those reading Arts subjects should be about 50:50 and that of postgraduates to undergraduates should be about 25:75. It also had mention of mature women.

Officers, was coming to an end in March 1978. The second grant from the Calouste Gulbenkian Fund for research awards was also finishing. I had made it known that I would retire from the Presidency at the end of September 1979 when I should have reached the University retiring age then of 67 (though the College retiring age was 70). The Bursar also was considering retirement. Fortunately the Appeal was going ahead steadily, our property was secure, the number of our applications for places from potential undergraduates was high and our examination results continued to be satisfactory. All this was good, but there was widespread agreement that we needed to replace the benefactions from the Cadbury Trust and Gulbenkian Foundation which we had enjoyed for so long. Both of these bodies had said that grants would not be given again for the same purpose as before, but that an application for a different project just possibly might be considered.

Since salaries, particularly for those primarily teaching for the College, were much needed, we sent to the Gulbenkian Foundation a request for a grant of £5,000 for a Teaching Fund. Despite what he described as an "excellently prepared application", the Secretary, in April 1978, had to let us know that his Trustees could not support it. This was not unexpected since they had already given us a second grant, contrary to their normal practice. Fortunately at this stage King's College generously promised us £3,000 per annum for three years which enabled us to continue making research awards.

The approach to the Cadbury Trust was much more complicated and discussions continued over many months. Ever since 1967 the Cadbury Trustees had given us their support and we believed that they were still interested in our progress. However, we accepted the fact that they were not primarily an educational fund, but one which had concern for "the social implications of the work of the College as a unique attempt to meet the needs of older women". We also accepted that their funds were essentially pump-priming and not for long-term support. Nonetheless, we decided to try once more and various suggestions were made. These included the possibility of developing within the College some kind of Public Relations Centre to investigate the "opportunities for the advancement of women in general and our own members in particular", and to augment the support for those, both inside the College and outside, "who wish to enter late or return to professional, or managerial life"[103]. This proposal met with considerable interest, but the Governing Body considered that our greatest need was finance to forward our aims and plans already specified in our Appeal literature. We therefore decided to ask again, but on a smaller scale, for help with our Appeal. Sadly, as we feared, the Trustees of the Cadbury Trust were unable to respond to our application and for the first time we faced the future without their help. They certainly had played a most important part in the development of the College for which we were deeply grateful.

103 The idea of such a Centre came from Margaret Braithwaite. She thought that use could be made of the studies carried out in the preparation of the Appeal literature.

Again and again the minutes of meetings show that the College was determined to do all it could to become an Approved Foundation as soon as possible. To do this, as mentioned above, the most important matter was the raising of further funds so the Appeal continued vigorously along the lines laid out in the Development Plan. Other fund-raising activities organised by individual members of the College included a ball,[104] held at the University Centre in December 1979, which was much enjoyed and provided a considerable sum of money (at least £1,700). Later a fashion show, despite the doubts of some as to its suitability, was displayed in the Hall of King's College and raised a further £1,000.

Some money as well as interest in the College was also raised by letting residential rooms to University visitors and for many years housing a summer school of archaeologists. On several occasions a refresher course for solicitors was held in the College in the vacation. This very successful venture was initiated by one of our Fellows (Jillinda Tiley) and was truly in the spirit of the College for it helped both women and men who, for one reason or another, needed to be brought up to date in their subject.

During the many discussions on the constitution, mention was made on several occasions of the possibility of including men as well as women in the College. The main reasons why this was thought to be inappropriate were several. Perhaps the most important was that all the money we had so far received had been given to us as an institution for women. It was also an institution with a particular concern for those who had had an interruption or a change of direction in their careers, a situation much more common among women than among men. Also to go co-residential would make the College less effective in increasing the proportion of women in the University.

One of the main pre-occupations of the year 1978/79 was the finding of a new Bursar and President. Joyce Linfoot had held the office of Bursar since 1967 and had been Secretary to the Trustees since 1970. She had worked very hard and the College owes her a great debt of gratitude for her determination that Lucy Cavendish should secure its premises and endowment rather than satisfy all the many requests made for current purposes. Her successor as Bursar was Ellen Macintosh who took office in January 1979 and continues there to this day. I much enjoyed working with her during my last two terms.

I retired at the end of September 1979 after nine years as President. I am immensely grateful to the College for giving me this honour and with it the opportunity to take part in so much that was interesting and exhilarating. I was only sorry that we had not yet achieved Approved Foundation status which I then believed to be not very far away. In all other ways I thoroughly enjoyed almost all of it.

The details of the election of the new President I know little about since

104 Evelyn Povey was the main organizer of this ball.

custom dictates that one President does not take part in the selection of another. The matter was in the hands of the then Vice-President, Hilda Davidson, and the Governing Body. The result was that the Lady Bowden, formerly an Under Secretary in the Department of Trade and Industry, was elected my successor.

Postscript

On retirement as President, I went to live in Sussex, but at the request of the new President, I remained a Trustee until May 1982. I had originally intended to finish my account at this point, thinking that the next five years would best be described by someone who was still more closely involved in Lucy Cavendish affairs during this period. However I was pressed to continue the story up to the time when the College achieved Approved Foundation status. I therefore, as before, studied the minutes of the Trustees' and other meetings, but minutes when one has not been present at the time are much less revealing than when one has taken part. I then came to the conclusion that the best course was for me to give a brief outline only of the more important matters, and I am indebted to my successor for some of the content of these concluding paragraphs.

Phyllis Bowden, (now Mrs.Hetzel), became President on 1st October 1979, a time when Universities faced two major problems: a reduction in government financial support and inevitable decline in the numbers of school-leaving students. The University Treasurer, during the summer of 1979, had told all Colleges that Cambridge University would have to make substantial economies as a result of the cut of £9 million imposed on University Grant Committee funds by the Government. The Vice Chancellor also warned that the number of undergraduates admitted to the University in October 1980 might have to be restricted to 94% of the number admitted the year before.

Having taken advice from the Vice-Chancellor and the chief University Officers, the new President considered that Lucy Cavendish should concentrate its main energies on becoming an Approved Foundation as soon as possible. The preparation of an application asking the University to allow a change of status was started at once. The document was completed by December 1980 and was sent, with the agreement of the Trustees, to the Registrary. The material was comprehensive and included a general account of the College and its history and notes on its buildings and administration, its academic profile, its Fellowship, and its "draft provisional statutes." A covering letter from the President[105] explained that the statutes had been derived from a set of

105 Phyllis Hetzel adds that it was a pity that only the cover reached the Council of the Senate.

working regulations which had been agreed over the years and which would continue to guide the day by day working of the College.

In February 1981 the College was informed that the uncertainties in the general University situation made it necessary to defer further consideration of the application for about a year. In fact these uncertainties continued and it was three years before the University made its response. During this period there was much correspondence and discussion between the College and the Registrary. Further information and clarification was provided and advice sought of many senior people, particularly an adviser to the Council of the Senate on Statutes.[106]

One of the important matters to be resolved was the extent to which the Trustees were still responsible for the government of the College. Following the terms of the original Trust Deed they agreed that they should continue to hold the College's endowment, freehold and property, but could hand over more and more of the management of its affairs to the Governing Body. This process was completed and on 12th January 1982 they formally delegated the government of the College to the President and Fellows.

Another question relating to the government of the College was the constitutional position of the Senior Members. Phyllis Bowden writes "The College was advised that it might be undesirable to keep scholars as Senior Members without clearer definition of their rights and obligations. It was therefore decided to abolish the title and offer those who held it membership rights for life, rather than for a limited tenure. A new status of Fellow Commoner was established at the same time." Sadly some Senior Members found the new circumstances unacceptable and resigned from active membership of the College.

The College was also advised by the Registrary to seek a Visitor, an office customarily found in statutes of Cambridge Colleges. The functions of the Visitor are partly ceremonial and partly to act as an independent judge should there ever be serious dispute within the Fellowship. In the early days of Lucy Cavendish it was thought that this function, if ever needed, could be performed by the Trustees, but the time had come for a more formal arrangement. The College, with the agreement of the University, then invited the Chancellor, H.R.H. the Duke of Edinburgh, if he would honour the College by becoming its Visitor. His acceptance gave truly great pleasure and encouragement.

Two other topics were of vital importance: finance and student numbers. On the money front it was obvious that the College's hopes would not be realized unless its finances were sound and of sufficiently large dimensions. For this reason Phyllis Bowden also concentrated at once on an appeal. A London-based appeal committee was set up, much hard work was done and

---

106 The adviser was Mr.Yale and Phyllis Hetzel says that his generosity, and that of other Senior members of the University cannot be too warmly appreciated.

a satisfactory sum of money was raised, including the first large individual benefaction of £100,000 from an anonymous donor. The generosity of all the donors, together with three legacies of houses from past Fellows made it possible for the College to allay the Council of the Senate's misgivings on financial viability.

In organising the appeal, the President made many new outside contacts which brought valuable publicity to the College and in turn led to an increasing number of applications for student places. This fact was important in the negotiations on the number of undergraduates, other than those from overseas, the College could admit under the special quota scheme imposed by the University as a result of financial cuts. This threatened Lucy Cavendish seriously, for a small institution cannot survive if it loses a significant proportion of its fee-paying students. However agreement was reached and the number of undergraduates never had to drop below 46.

During the course of so much consultation, it was suggested that the President should seek election to the Council of the Senate. This she did and at her first meeting of the Council in January 1983 it came as somewhat of a shock to find among the papers a recommendation to the Council to turn down Lucy Cavendish's application. More time was sought, more advice was taken. Some members of the Council were exercised not only about money and student numbers, but on the continuing need for a single sex College, even for such a clearly defined category of mature women students and scholars. She adds that three times she waited in the Octagon Room while the College's case was discussed. It says much for the worth of the cause that in July 1984 the Council of the Senate published its long awaited report which contained the recommendation that the College should be recognized as an Approved Foundation. (Reporter 1983/4.p.710) This appeared in the long vacation so a long wait in suspense had to be endured before the subject could come to a University Discussion in the Michaelmas Term. Although one member of Council[107] expressed some doubt during the Discussion about the wisdom of the University taking on more responsibilities in times of financial stringency, no opposition developed and no ballot was called. The necessary Grace was passed on 10th November and the President was able to report at the Annual Dinner on that evening that we were now, at long last, an Approved Foundation within the University of Cambridge. This was greeted with great enthusiasm and she was warmly congratulated on her part in its achievement.

That Annual Dinner of 1984 was also a farewell dinner for the President for she had told the College in May that she intended to retire at the end of the Michaelmas term, after rather more than 5 years in office. The large number of members present at the dinner wished her well in her re-marriage and her life in California as Mrs. Hetzel.

107 The single speaker was Dr.George Reid.

POSTSCRIPT

With the departure of Phyllis Bowden, Doris Thoday, who had been elected Vice-President in November 1980, became Acting President while a new President was being sought. To her befell the task of arranging the occasion on June 12 1985 when the newly appointed Visitor, H.R.H. the Duke of Edinburgh, came to see the College. He toured the buildings, met many of the members and planted a tree. It was altogether a happy and memorable occasion and the Acting President was congratulated on the highly professional way in which it had been organised. That visit will be the only one that the Visitor will make to the College under its first legal name of Lucy Cavendish Collegiate Society, for early in 1986 its request to be known officially as Lucy Cavendish College was granted by the University. (Reporter,1985/6 p.229).

In July 1985 the College announced that it had elected as President Dame Anne Warburton, then U.K. British Representative at the United Nations in Geneva and formerly British Ambassador in Denmark. She took up office in November 1985 and the College started a new stage of development with a higher status in the University, an improved name and a new leader. Lucy Cavendish had chosen two biologists and a Senior Civil Servant as Presidents and had now welcomed a diplomat.

APPENDIX I.

THE GOVERNMENT OF THE UNIVERSITY.
From The Cambridge University Handbook (C.U.P.). 1986/7.

p.1. 1. THE UNIVERSITY.

The University is a self-governing body; the legislative authority is the Regent House, which consists mainly of the teaching and administrative staff of the University and Colleges. The Senate, which consists of all holders of the M.A. or higher degrees, has now only certain formal duties, other than meeting for the discussion of Reports made by the Council of the Senate and other bodies. The chief administrative body of the University is the Council of the Senate, which is elected by the Regent House. The General Board of the Faculties co-ordinates the educational policy of the University and the Financial Board supervises its financial affairs.

The nominal and ceremonial head of the University is the Chancellor, who is elected for life. The Vice-Chancellor is a head of a College who is nominated for election by the Council of the Senate and normally holds office for two years. He presides over Congregations of the Regent House, at which degrees are conferred, and is Chairman of the Council of the Senate and the more important of the many Boards and Syndicates which manage the affairs of the University.

Changes in the Ordinances, or Regulations, of the University are proposed by the Board or Syndicate concerned in the form of reports which, after being approved for publication by the Council of the Senate, are published in the *Cambridge University Reporter*. Such reports can be commented on by members of the Senate at Discussions which are held once a fortnight in Full Term. A report may be amended after remarks made in a Discussion. Subsequently a Grace, which is a motion for the approval of recommendations made in a report, is submitted to a vote in the Regent House. Minor amendments of Ordinances are proposed in Graces which the Council of the Senate submit for the approval of the Regent House without the formality of Report and discussion. Ordinances may not infringe the University Statutes. The procedure for making amendments of the Statutes is the same as for the Ordinances, but such amendments require the approval of the Queen in Council, after the approval of the Regent House has been obtained.

The educational and research activities of the University are organized in Faculties, some of which are subdivided into Departments. All are answerable to the General Board of the Faculties. Through the Faculties, the University is responsible for lectures and laboratory work. The University also conducts all examinations and awards degrees; but it is the Colleges which select students for admission, arrange the tuition of undergraduates either individually or in small groups, and see to the welfare, both academic and personal, of undergraduates. All undergraduates admitted by the Colleges must however satisfy the University's matriculation requirements.

p.9. *MATRICULATION*

Matriculation marks the formal admission of a student to membership of the University, and a College may not allow an unmatriculated student *in statu pupillari* to remain in residence after the division of his first term. Every candidate for matriculation must subscribe to the following declaration by signing the Matriculation

Registrarion Form: I promise to observe the Statutes and Ordinances of the University as far as they concern me, and to pay due respect and obedience to the Chancellor and other officers of the University.

Note The Registrary is the Administrative Officer whose duties include acting as Secretary to the Council of the Senate and as Editor of the *University Reporter*. He is appointed by the Council.

APPENDIX II.

Vice-Chancellors of Cambridge University since 1950

1951 Lionel Ernest Howard Whitby Downing College
1953 Henry Urmston Willink Magdalene College
1955 Brian Westerdale Downs Christ's College
1957 Edgar Douglas Adrian Trinity College
1959 Herbert Butterfield Peterhouse
1961 William Ivor Jennings Trinity Hall
1963 John Sandwith Boys Smith St.John's College
1965 Arthur Llewellyn Armitage Queens' College
1967 Eric Ashby Clare College
1969 William Owen Chadwick Selwyn College
1971 William Alexander Deer Trinity Hall
1973 John Wilfred Linnett Sidney Sussex
1975 Alice Rosemary Murray New Hall
1977 Alan Howard Cottrell Jesus College
1979 Peter Swinnerton-Dyer St.Catharine's College
1981 Francis Harry Hinsley St.John's College
1983 John Butterfield Downing College
1985 Richard Hume Adrian Pembroke College

APPENDIX III

Collegiate Institutions in the University established or recognized since 1950.

Based on Cambridge Annual Register (Historical Supplements)

1954 *New Hall.* An Association to promote a Third Foundation for Women in the University of Cambridge was formed in 1953. In 1954 a Company, named New Hall, Cambridge was incorporated and became a Recognized Institution. In 1965 it became an Approved Foundation and in 1972 received its Royal Charter.

1960 *Churchill College.* A Trust was set up in 1958 to receive public subscriptions to establish a College in Canbridge as a memorial to Winston Churchill. Intended to be largely,but not wholly, devoted to Mathematics, Engineering and Natural Sciences. Generous response from private persons and industry for buildings and endowments. The Master and some Fellows were appointed by the Trustees. Briefly an Approved Foundation and then received its Royal Charter in 1960.

1964 *Darwin College.* Established as a collegiate society under Trust Deed by the Master and Fellows of Gonvillle and Caius, St.John's and Trinity Colleges. First

Recognized as an Approved Foundation and then received its Royal Charter in 1976. (First funds came from the parent Colleges and the Max Rayne Foundation).

1965 *Wolfson College.* Founded as University College under Trust Deed between the Chancellor, Masters and Scholars of the University of Cambridge and five Trustees for research, especially among officers and graduates of the University. Reserved Fellowships for University officers nominated by the University. First recognized as an Approved Foundation in 1976 and then received its Royal Charter in 1977. The name was changed after a grant from the Wolfson Foundation in 1973. (First funds came from the University).

1965 *Lucy Cavendish Collegiate Society.* Recognized as an Approved Society under a Trust Deed executed on 15.9.1965. Trustees delegated powers of government to the Governing Body in 1982 and in 1984 it became an Approved Foundation. In 1986 the name was changed to Lucy Cavendish College.

1965 *Clare Hall.* Established by Clare College under a Trust Deed. Endowments and benefactions from Ford and Old Dominion Foundations with the particular object of enabling scholars from outside Cambridge to be invited into Visiting Fellowships. Became an Approved Foundation in 1966 and received its Royal Charter in 1984.

1965 *Elizabeth Phillips Hughes Hall.* Formerly a Recognized Institution of the University which had originally been founded in 1885 for the training of women graduates intending to follow the profession of teaching. Became an Approved Society in 1965 and an Approved Foundation in 1985.

1965 *St.Edmund's House.* Originally founded by 15th Duke of Norfolk and established under a Roman Catholic Trust in 1898. Recognized as an Approved Society in 1965 and an Approved Foundation in 1985.

1966 *Fitzwilliam College.* Originally started for Non-Collegiate Students, it became first an Approved Foundation and fully collegiate in 1966.

1977 *Robinson College.* Foundation entirely due to the munificence of Mr.David Robinson. The object of the Trust Deed signed by him and Trustees in 1973 was the advancement of education, learning and research by founding a Collegiate Society for both male and female members of the University. Recognized as Approved Foundation in 1977 and received its Royal Charter in' 1984.

1977 *Homerton College.* An Approved Society within the College was recognized for those candidates reading for any examination leading to the degree of B.Ed. after two years study in the College.

APPENDIX IV.

The Colleges and other Collegiate Societies.

The Colleges.

There are 27 fully self-governing Colleges in Cambridge. The control of the affairs of each rests with the Head and Fellows or, in some Colleges, with a smaller executive body elected by them from among themselves. All these Colleges have been granted, by the Sovereign, a Royal Charter which confers on them certain privileges and functions. They also have, however, obligations to the University including those concerned with finance. These obligations are defined in Statute G of the University Statutes and include the statement that every College in the University shall make a yearly contribution out of its revenues to the University. Since 1966, following the report of the Bridges Syndicate, a proportion of these contributions pass into the Colleges' Fund from which grants can be made to some of the poorer Colleges.

Other Collegiate Societies.

There are also 2 other categories of institutions recognized by the University under the provisions of Statute H. These institutions are: *Approved Foundations* whose status differs from that of a self-governing College in several limiting respects, for example their Heads are not eligible for nomination as Vice-Chancellor. However Approved Foundations are eligible to apply for grants from the Colleges' Fund, though they are not required to contribute to this fund during their first 10 years.

At present St.Edmund's College, Lucy Cavendish College and Hughes Hall are within this category. *Approved Societies* which are institutions of a less formal and more experimental character than is implied by an Approved Foundation. They are not eligible to apply to the Colleges' Fund. Homerton College is at present the sole representative.

Formerly there was a third category, *Recognized Institution for Women*, but this was abolished in 1964.

APPENDIX V.

Trustees.

Those signing the Trust Deed of 15 September 1965 were: Lord Annan, O.B.E. Provost of King's College, Cambridge, later Provost of University College, London. Dr.Anna M.Bidder, Curator of Malacology, Museum of Zoology, University of Cambridge. Mrs.Margaret F.S.Bottrall, University Lecturer in the Department of Education, Tutor of Hughes Hall, Cambridge. Mrs. Margaret M.Braithwaite (Masterman), Director of the Cambridge Language Research Unit. Mr.W.A.Camps, University Lecturer in Classics, Fellow and later Master of Pembroke College. The Right Rev. Bishop George A.Chase, Fellow of Selwyn College, formerly Bishop of Ripon. Professor Sir Joseph B.Hutchinson, F.R.S. Drapers Professor of Agriculture, Fellow of St.John's College. Dr.Nora K.Willson, Principal Lecturer and Head of French Department, Homerton College, Cambridge.

Those subsequently appointed were: 1966 Mr.C.W.Crawley, Fellow and later Hon.Fellow of Trinity Hall. Resigned 1978. (Chairman of Trustees 1969 to 1975) 1967 Sir Gordon Sutherland, F.R.S. Master of Emmanuel College. Resigned 1969. 1969 Mr.B.W.Farmer, Then President of St.John's College. Director, Centre South Asia Studies. 1970 Dr.C.Kate Bertram, President of Lucy Cavendish College, Resigned 1982. 1970 Sir Eric Ashby, F.R.S. Master of Clare College. Resigned 1975. 1974 Mr.J.R.S.Walker, Chief Engineer, Rugby Cement Company. Resigned 1978, 1975 Prof.Alistair N.Worden. Chairman, Huntingdon Research Centre. Fellow of Wolfson College. Died 1987. 1975 Sir Robert Cockburn, KBE, CB. Churchill College, Chairman of National Computing Centre. Resigned 1985. 1975 Professor Dorothy M.Emmet, formerly Professor of Philosophy University of Manchester, Hon.Fellow, Lady Margaret

Hall, Oxford. Resigned 1986. 1978 Mrs.Dorothy Hahn, Bursar of Newnham College, Resigned 1983. 1978 Professor W.R.Niblett, CBE. Prof.Higher Education, London. Resigned 1982. 1979 Sir Alan Cottrell,F.R.S. Master of Jesus College. (Chairman of Trustees 1980-86) 1980 Sir Peter Thornton, KCB. Director Courtaulds and Laird Group; Permanent Secretary. Department of Trade, 1974-1977. 1980 Professor Violet Cane. Prof.Mathematical Statistics, Manchester 1980 Mr.Deryck Mumford, CBE. Formerly Principal of CCAT. 1984 Miss Sheila Browne, CB, Principal of Newnham College. Formerly Senior Chief Inspector, Secondary Education. 1986 Mr.David P. Thomson, Director-General, British Invisible Exports Council. 1986 Sir John, now Lord, Butterfield, OBE. Master of Downing College. Regius Professor of Physic, Cambridge.(Chairman of Trustees 1986).

N.B. Margaret Bottrall was Acting Chairman of Trustees 1975-80.

APPENDIX VI.

Founding Fellows appointed by the Trustees in 1965.

BERTRAM. Mrs C. Kate, MA. PhD.
BOTTRALL, Mrs Margaret, F.S, MA, Resigned 1971 on appointment as Tutor of Hughes Hall.
BRAITHWAITE, Mrs Margaret, M. MA, Director of Cambridge Language Research Unit.
CLEGG, Mrs Marion J. MA.
CLIFFORD, Mrs M.Eileen L, MA.
EVANS, Mrs Jessie M, MA.
GILES, Miss Phyllis M, MA. Librarian, Fitzwilliam Museum, Cambridge.
GOODY, Mrs Esther N, MA PhD. Resigned 1976 to become Fellow of New Hall.
HOLMES, Mrs Barbara E, MA. PhD.
JOYSEY, Mrs Valerie C, BSc(London), MA. PhD. Technical Officer, Department of Pathology, Cambridge.
KEILIN, (Mrs Whiteley) Joan E. MB. BChir. MA. Ph.D. Resigned on moving to Oxford.
LARTER, Miss Julie E.I. BA(London) MA. Librarian, Scientific Periodicals, Cambridge.
LINDGREN-UTSI, Mrs Ethel J, MA. Ph.D. Hon.Secretary,Reindeer Council of the U.K.
LINFOOT, Mrs Joyce J, MA. Lecturer, Department of Education, Cambridge.
LIVERSIDGE, Miss Joan E.A. MLitt. FSA. Hon. Keeper Roman Collections, Museum Archaeology & Ethnology, Cambridge & Recognized Lecturer in Archaeology.
LU, Miss Gwei-Djen, BA(Nanking) PhD.
NEEDHAM, Mrs Dorothy, ScD, F.R.S.
PETRIE, Mrs Ann, MA. Resigned 1966 on leaving Cambridge.
WALLACE, Mrs Margaret, MA. PhD. University Teaching Officer in Department of Genetics, Cambridge, & Assistant Director in Research.
WILLSON, Miss Nora K. MA. Ph.D. Principal Lecturer & Head of French Department, Homerton College, Cambridge.
WOOD-LEGH, Miss Kathleen L. BLitt(Oxon), MA(McGill), LittD.

APPENDIX VII.

THE EXTENT OF INFLATION BETWEEN 1950 AND 1987.

Information kindly provided by Mrs.Ellen Mackintosh, the Bursar of the College.

The Retail Price Index, on a chain base from 1950, shows prices to have risen approximately thirteen fold by 1987. Of course, the goods available have changed during that time, so this is only a very rough approximation of the extent of inflation. Nevertheless, it gives an indication of the order of magnitude involved.

INDICES

Suppose 1950 = 100

then from 1950 to 1956 prices went up from 113 to 153, or 35% 1956 = 135
from 1956 to 1962 prices went up from 102 to 117.5, or 15%, 1962 = 155
from 1962 to 1974 prices went up from 100 to 208.2, or 108%, 1974 = 323
from 1974 to 1987 prices went up from 100 to, say, 400, or 300% 1987 = 1292
(Figures based on the UK Annual Abstract of Statistics).

Index